RECIPES TO REMEMBER

FROM OUR FAMILY

Jock was a chef who left his work kitchen behind each day and happily came home to our family kitchen. Soon after we first met, I found my position sitting at the kitchen bench next to Ava, sipping wine while he cooked for us. And as our family grew, he started teaching our little ones the ropes with the same focus and passion that defined him.

On the weekends our home was his favourite place to be – kitchen chaos, meal planning, spontaneous trips to the markets, and last-minute changes of mind. Every Saturday and Sunday, there he would be in his navy dressing gown, his curly hair dishevelled, standing at the stove or coffee machine with Alfie by his side. No matter what he was doing in the kitchen, it was always to look after us. Food was his love language.

Jock would bring me my coffee in bed; he would have our little ones dressed and on their stools in the kitchen, next to him, with Scottish ballads playing loudly. The kids would be sipping on their own 'coffee milk' (don't panic, it was just a glass of froth) watching their Papa move around the kitchen. Only recently, I made a coffee for myself before the kids woke up, and Isla came quietly downstairs and into the kitchen and said, 'I could smell coffee, I thought Papa was home.'

The sound of the coffee grinder, the quiet swiping of the Berkel slicer – these small familiar noises trick me, for the most fleeting of moments, into thinking that Jock is still here with us. What I wouldn't do for one more moment with him, even if it was just watching him cook one more time.

After we lost Jock, I wanted to work on projects that had meaning and left a genuine legacy of the extraordinary person who was the centre of our world. Something his children could hold and be proud of. This cookbook, filled with his favourite recipes, was at the top of my list. To decide which recipes to include, I first went to our memories as a family – meals we would ask for on our birthdays, the ones he made with the kids, and what he loved to make for friends who dropped in unexpectedly. Those are the recipes we've chosen to share with you here.

Food brought Jock so much joy; it gave him focus as a young man, and it gave him purpose throughout his life. And that is why we made the decision to share his recipes. This cookbook is a celebration of the fun Jock would have in the kitchen. It was also fun to bring this book to life, and I hope you feel the same as you start cooking from it.

From the kids and me: thank you for wanting to keep a piece of Jock in your home and for helping us keep his legacy alive. As you make his recipes for the people you care about, hold them that little bit closer. Because, as we've heartbreakingly learnt, sometimes life can be far too short.

— *Loz, Ava, Alfie and Isla xxx*

FOREWORD
JAMIE OLIVER

With a big smile on my face and a tear in my eye, it's my honour to write this foreword for the legendary Jock Zonfrillo. This gorgeous collection of personal family recipes is an incredible way for us all to celebrate a wonderful chef, human being, husband, father, friend, and for many, an iconic judge on *MasterChef Australia*.

With love, grit, determination and celebration, Lauren Zonfrillo has masterfully collated and curated this beautifully intimate family cookbook of Jock's most loved and, as yet, unpublished recipes.

Paying homage to both his Scottish and Italian roots, this is a book full of recipes you'll want to make and eat. From the simple staples that will make your meals sing, like pickles, oils, sauces and salsas; to his favourite home dinners (sign me up for a limoncello chicken traybake), you can sense on every page that Jock used food as a love letter to nourish his family, friends and customers.

These dishes are a real snapshot of not just a talented and genius chef, but, more importantly, a homeboy, husband and dad. You can really feel the connection to cherished moments and precious memories, and I know he would love you to replicate these occasions with your own loved ones.

I first met Jock way back in the early days of *The Naked Chef,* when he was a 22-year-old head chef at the beautiful Tresanton Hotel in Cornwall. Young, handsome, laser-focused and hungry to learn, he was already battle-hardened, having worked in Michelin-starred restaurants in London under the likes of Marco Pierre White, and achieved status as young Scottish Chef of the Year at the ripe age of 16. Without question, I knew I was in the presence of a legend in the making.

Not long after, Jock went on to work and reside in his beloved Australia, quickly making his presence felt with his great cooking talent, and through his curiosity and dedication to honouring Indigenous Australian ingredients. He found his culinary home when he opened his restaurant, Orana, and his ability to build loyal teams and inspire others led to several industry awards – testament to his fresh and innovative approach to cooking, one that had a deep respect for native food and First Nations culture and traditions.

This book is a true celebration of Jock's life. It's his greatest hits and a glowing love of food and family. I implore you to flip through the book, pick a recipe that feels right for you in that moment, and channel Jock's spirit and sense of humour, creativity, warmth, and that overriding sense of care for the shopping, cooking, serving, table and atmosphere. He was all about that care for every last detail and sharing the love with people that matter to you. He would be really chuffed to know he'd inspired people to create those moments with their loved ones. And maybe, just maybe, you have a wee dram at the end and a toast to Jock and his beautiful family, carrying on his legacy through food.

Credit: Painted by Daniel Butterworth

Jock Zonfrillo

RECIPES TO REMEMBER

SIMON & SCHUSTER

New York · Amsterdam/Antwerp · London · Toronto · Sydney · New Delhi

CONTENTS

From our Family 3

Foreword by Jamie Oliver 5

FRIDGE AND PANTRY STAPLES	11
BREAKFAST CLASSICS	37
JOCK'S REGULARS	71
SNACKS AND COCKTAILS	103
QUICK AND BASIC	133
POSH SALADS	163
BARBECUE AND WOODFIRED	191
DESSERTS	215
RECIPES JOCK NICKED	243

Index 267

Fridge and PANTRY STAPLES

5-MINUTE CRISPY CHILLI OIL

MAKES 2 JARS

2 cups (500 ml) peanut oil
2 star anise
2 cinnamon sticks
2 brown cardamom pods, smashed
2 thumbs (40 g) ginger, peeled and finely diced
1 cup (80 g) chilli flakes
2½ tsp (4 g) Sichuan peppercorns
3 tsp (15 g) fermented black beans
6 garlic cloves, minced
3 tsp (15 g) mushroom powder
2¼ tbsp (20 g) sesame seeds
¼ cup (30 g) roasted peanuts, crushed
⅓ cup (80 ml) fish sauce
¼ cup (60 ml) dark soy sauce

Place the oil in a heavy-based saucepan with the star anise, cinnamon, brown cardamom and ginger. Heat the oil to 180°C then pick out the whole spices and discard.

Place the chilli flakes, peppercorns, black beans, garlic, mushroom powder, sesame seeds and peanuts in a large, heatproof bowl. Use a much larger bowl than you think as it can bubble up when you pour the hot oil over it. Pour over the hot oil, stirring ferociously. Add the fish sauce and soy sauce and mix well.

Let it cool slightly, then pour the oil into an airtight jar or bottle. It will keep in the fridge for up to 12 months, but you'll finish it well before then!

'This is the fast track to packing a chilli punch into your dish. Dumplings, scrambled eggs, pizza, pasta – you name the food and I'll most likely suggest you add a drizzle of this oil!'

BREAD AND BUTTER PICKLES

MAKES 1 X 750 ML JAR

750 g lebanese cucumbers, sliced 5 mm thick
½ brown onion, thinly sliced
3½ tbsp (75 g) fine sea salt
½ tsp coriander seeds
½ tsp yellow mustard seeds
¼ tsp black mustard seeds
¼ tsp turmeric powder
½ cup (125 ml) apple cider vinegar
½ cup (125 ml) rice wine vinegar
¼ cup (60 g) caster sugar

Combine the cucumber, onion and salt in a large bowl and let stand for 1 hour to draw out most of the moisture, mixing every 15 minutes or so.

Meanwhile, toast the coriander and yellow and black mustard seeds in a dry pan until aromatic. Let them cool slightly, then crush in a mortar and pestle. (#exercise!)

Place the crushed seeds in a saucepan with the turmeric, vinegars and sugar. Bring to a boil, then remove from heat and leave the pickling liquid to infuse.

Thoroughly rinse the cucumber and onion, then pat dry to remove any excess moisture. If you've got one, a salad spinner works really well for this.

Tightly pack the cucumber and onion into a clean, sterilised 750 ml jar. Bring the pickling liquid back to a simmer, then strain into the jar, ensuring it covers the pickles.

Allow the pickles to cool to room temperature before sealing the lid, then let stand at least overnight before serving.

'Every home needs a huge jar of these in the fridge, big enough to put your hand into for easier snacking.'

BRANSTON PICKLE

MAKES 2½ CUPS

½ cup (90 g) dates, seeds removed, roughly chopped
1¼ tbsp molasses
1¼ tbsp dark soy sauce
1¼ tbsp dark brown sugar
2 cups (500 ml) malt vinegar
3 tsp tomato paste
3 tsp Vegemite
¼ tsp black pepper
¼ tsp allspice
1 tsp mustard powder
1 tsp salt
1 tsp cornflour, dissolved in 1½ tsp cold water
1 carrot, diced into 1 cm cubes
1 swede, diced into 1 cm cubes
1 brown onion, diced into 1 cm cubes
1 Granny Smith apple, diced into 1 cm cubes

Combine the dates, molasses, soy sauce, sugar, vinegar, tomato paste, Vegemite, pepper, allspice, mustard powder and salt in a pot over high heat.

Bring the mixture to a boil, then simmer, stirring often, until it has reduced by half.

Grab your stick blender and blend until the mixture is completely smooth, then pass through a fine mesh strainer before returning to the pot.

Stream in the cornflour and whisk thoroughly.

Return the mixture to a boil, then add the carrot, swede, onion and apple. Boil until they are al dente, which should take about 2–3 minutes.

Remove from the heat and allow the pickle to cool fully before portioning into sterilised jars.

'There isn't a sandwich that isn't made a million times better with a thick layer of pickles.'

Jock eating his beloved mortadella panino with Bel Paese somewhere off the Amalfi Coast, Italy, July 2018.
Credit: Lauren Zonfrillo

'My first memory of the joy of food is holding Nonno's hand and toddling into the beautiful chaos of Fazzi's Italian deli in Glasgow. The smell hit me before my eyes took anything in, and I can still call it up: fresh focaccia, salami, parmesan — and beneath it all, the whiff of garlic, spice and briny olives. It blew my mind. Everything changed for me after that, in the best possible way.'

SUPER-SIMPLE HOMEMADE RICOTTA

MAKES 500 G

8 cups (2 litres) high-quality full-cream milk
1 tbsp table salt
⅔ cup (165 ml) white vinegar

Heat the milk in a heavy-based pot over low heat, stirring often to avoid scorching, until it reaches 86°C. Take this slow, give it a stir here and there, and don't walk away or there's a good chance it will catch on the bottom of the pan.

Add the salt and vinegar and stir gently to combine. You will see curds beginning to form. This is the good bit – you'll be tempted to poke at it but don't do that, just let it do it's thing.

Continue cooking the mixture over low heat until the milk reaches 90°C, then remove from the heat and leave for 20 minutes. Scoop the curds into ricotta moulds or a cheesecloth-lined bowl and allow the whey to drain away for an hour or two (the length of time you allow here depends on how dry you like your ricotta).

Reward yourself with a little spoonful to taste it, then pop it into an airtight container in the fridge.

You can add it to sandwiches, stir it through pasta, or plate up like the picture opposite with peas, mushrooms and thyme.

SALSA VERDE

MAKES 1 CUP

1 large bunch flat-leaf parsley, leaves picked (about 40 g)
1 bunch basil, leaves picked (about 30 g)
¼ bunch mint, leaves picked (about 15 g)
1 small garlic clove
3 tbsp (60 g) baby capers, rinsed and dried
3 tbsp (30 g) anchovies
½ cup (125 ml) extra-virgin olive oil
2 tbsp red wine vinegar
1 tbsp lemon juice
1½ tbsp dijon mustard

Place all ingredients in a blender or food processor and blend to a smooth sauce. Season with salt and pepper and you're good to go!

You're aiming for something that looks messy but tastes like it came from a trattoria with a view.

CAFE DE PARIS BUTTER

MAKES 1 LOG

- 2 tsp (10 g) hot Japanese curry paste
- 1 small eschalot, finely diced
- 1 garlic clove, minced
- zest of 1 lemon, plus 1¼ tbsp juice
- 2 egg yolks
- 1 tbsp (20 g) cornichons, finely chopped
- 2 tsp (10 g) capers, finely chopped
- 2 tbsp (25 g) anchovy fillets, finely chopped
- ½ tsp smoked paprika
- 1½ tbsp white soy sauce
- 2 tsp Worcestershire sauce
- 1½ tbsp dijon mustard
- 1 tbsp Armagnac
- ½ bunch (25 g) flat-leaf parsley, finely chopped
- 1 tsp finely chopped lemon thyme
- 2 tsp finely chopped thyme
- 250 g unsalted butter, softened
- 1 tbsp finely sliced chives

In a large mixing bowl, whisk the curry paste with a splash of hot water to dissolve it. Add all the remaining ingredients except the butter and chives, and give it a really ferocious whisk. It might look like a mess at this point – but stay with me, you're building a flavour bomb.

Add the butter and whisk to emulsify into the other ingredients – your butter being room temperature is the key to this working. Season with salt and pepper, but keep in mind where you think you will add this – if it's to steak, it's likely you would have seasoned the steak as you cooked it, so go lighter on the salt in this butter. Add the chives and fold them through the mixture.

Place a sheet of baking paper flat on the bench and use your spatula to scoop the butter onto the paper, shaping it roughly into a log.

Using the baking paper, roll it neatly into a smooth sausage-like shape, aiming to remove any air pockets by pressing the baking paper onto the butter. Twist the ends of the paper to seal it and boom, it's done!

Place the butter in the fridge to firm then it's ready to slice and serve.

'Sure, there are heaps of ingredients, so make this in bulk and store it in baking paper in the freezer.'

VEGAN 'FISH' SAUCE

MAKES 500 ML

1¼ cups (300 ml) water

¾ cup plus 1 tbsp (200 ml) seaweed kombu dashi

5 tbsp (100 ml) coconut vinegar

5 tbsp (100 ml) white soy sauce

200 g tamarind concentrate

200 ml coconut aminos

30 g dried shiitake mushrooms, broken into small pieces

10 g wakame

10 g kombu

This may be one of the easiest recipes you can make. Place all the ingredients in a large pot and bring to a very gentle simmer for about 30 minutes. Keep an eye on it – you don't want a rapid bubble or the reduction will happen too fast.

And guess what, you're done! Strain and pour the liquid into a sterilised bottle and pop it in the fridge or in the pantry. It will be OK to keep using for up to 12 months.

'I came up with this recipe after receiving sooo many requests for a "fish" sauce without the fish!

Fish sauce is a full whack of flavour; it fills your mouth with umami and it's really salty, so I took that as guidance when I made this. With just nine ingredients and half an hour of your time, you'll have your own shelf-stable vegan "fish" sauce.'

FRIDGE AND PANTRY STAPLES

SEMI-DRIED TOMATOES

MAKES 1 JAR

800 g baby Roma tomatoes

FOR THE PRESERVING OIL

1 cup (250 ml) extra-virgin olive oil

2 thyme sprigs

1 rosemary sprig

2 garlic cloves, smashed

This is sunshine in a jar and such a therapeutic task to do in the kitchen. Let's start with the preserving oil – combine the oil, herbs and garlic in a small saucepan and heat over a low heat until it reaches 110°C. If you don't have a thermometer, you'll know you've reached the right heat when the oil just begins to sizzle.

Remove from the heat and leave the oil to infuse with all the other ingredients until it has cooled to room temperature, then store in a sterilised glass bottle or jar in the fridge.

To make the semi-dried tomatoes, score the skin in a cross at the bottom of the toms, and place them cross up on a tray. Then you can choose to blowtorch them to blister the skins (I love this bit) or pour boiling water over them and let them soak for a minute, then place them into a bowl of ice water and peel. The skins should come away fairly easily. Take your time and enjoy the process.

Once the skins have been removed, be super gentle with your tomatoes and place them in a bowl and lightly coat with salt, pepper and a drizzle of the preserving oil. Then pop them on a baking tray lined with baking paper in a single layer and put them into the oven at 70°C for 7 hours while you listen to a few podcasts or mow the lawn. If your oven temperature gauge doesn't go that low, use the 'keep warm' setting.

When it's done, place in a sterilised preserving jar and cover with the remainder of the preserving oil making sure the tomatoes are fully submerged. These can live in the fridge for up to two weeks.

'If you can't lay these out in the sun all day like the Italians, this is a solid backup.'

SUGO AL POMODORO

MAKES 2-3 LITRES

1½ tbsp extra-virgin olive oil
6 garlic cloves
2 large white onions, finely diced
1 large bunch basil, leaves and stalks separated
6 x 400 g cans whole peeled tomatoes
6 tomatoes

Place a large, heavy-based pot over medium heat and add the olive oil. While that warms up, peel the garlic and give each clove a gentle squash with the side of your knife – enough to wake them up, but not obliterate them. Pop the garlic and onion into the pot and give it all a good stir so everything is covered with oil.

Now, throw in the basil stalks and season with a decent pinch of salt and stir again. You'll start to smell that lovely, herby base building already.

In the meantime, empty your tinned whole tomatoes into a big bowl. Take one of your fresh tomatoes and gently squeeze it so it bursts – this is not the time to be wearing white. Grate the rest of that tomato down to the skin and chuck the skin away. Repeat with the others.

Add all the tomatoes to the pot. As you go, squeeze the tinned ones through your fingers so they break up nicely – it's a bit messy, but that's half the fun. Give it a good stir and let the sauce simmer gently for about 15 minutes. Once it's had time to mellow and mingle, pick out the garlic and basil stalks and bin them – their work here is done.

Stir through the fresh basil leaves and have a taste. If it needs a touch more salt or pepper, now's the time. Turn off the heat and let the sauce sit. Once it's cooled down, spoon it into sterilised jars or airtight containers. They can keep in the fridge for up to a week or freeze it in batches.

'Everyone needs to know how to make sugo al pomodoro (Italian for tomato sauce) – it opens up a world of delicious possibilities. Go on now, start sugo-ing!'

HOMEMADE BUTTER

MAKES 300 G BUTTER AND 250 ML BUTTERMILK

600 ml thickened cream, chilled

½ tsp salt flakes (optional)

Pour the thickened cream into the bowl of a stand mixer fitted with a whisk attachment. Cover the bowl with cling film or a clean tea towel – it'll save you from redecorating the kitchen – and start whisking on medium speed.

Over the next 15 minutes, you'll see the cream go through a few stages. First, it'll whip up like cream normally does, then as it overwhips it will start to collapse into tiny yellow butterfat granules. This is where the magic begins. Eventually, you'll notice the cream fully split into golden butterfat and bright white buttermilk. When that happens, hit stop – fast. Trust me, you do not want buttermilk flying around your walls.

Pour off the buttermilk (save it if you like baking), and pop the butterfat back in the mixer for another quick churn until it fully comes together. Now you've got butter. But we're not done just yet.

Get your hands in there and gently squeeze out the rest of the buttermilk from the butter solid. Then give your butter a cold-water bath in a bowl of iced water. Keep kneading it gently in the water until the liquid runs clear then lift out your beautiful, golden butter and pat it dry.

If you want salted butter weigh it, then fold through 1% of its weight in salt. So for 300 grams, that's around 3 grams, or half a teaspoon. You can then shape your butter – if you've got butter paddles, now's their time to shine. Use them to press, shape, and give your butter that beautiful old-school texture. It's a wee bit of kitchen theatre but impressive when you put the butter on the table.

'There's nothing better than fresh bread and butter smeared on there so thick you can see your teeth marks when you bite into it.'

Credit: Lauren Zonfrillo

'Cooking gave me a way back to myself. It saved me. I could lose myself in a dish and come out the other side with something to show for it — something that made someone else happy. That's powerful.'

PESTO

MAKES 1 SMALL JAR

½ cup (75 g) pine nuts

½–1 garlic clove

1 bunch basil, leaves picked

½ cup (40 g) grated parmesan

⅔ cup extra-virgin olive oil

lemon juice, to taste (optional)

Toast the pine nuts in a frying pan over medium heat without any oil until they are lightly golden. Don't walk away and do other stuff while they toast, 'cause we all know they'll burn! Don't skip this toasting step; it makes all the difference to the flavour.

Place the toasted pine nuts, garlic, basil and parmesan in a blender or food processor and blitz away. Get it close to the consistency that you like, then stop and add the oil. If you have a blender or food processor that allows you to add it gradually, do that, if not, go all-in.

Once the oil is incorporated into the pesto, add salt and pepper to taste. When you're happy with that balance, you can add some lemon juice if that's your cup of tea.

Pour the pesto into a jar and put it somewhere in the fridge where you can see it so you don't forget to use it – it should last 2–4 weeks.

'You should make your pesto to your preferences – I like mine with less garlic than usual, lots of pepper, and a squeeze of lemon juice. If you want yours punchier and more traditional, go harder on the garlic and forget about the lemon shenanigans.'

BREAKFAST
Classics

BIRCHER PORRIDGE

SERVES 4

1 cup (100 g) rolled oats
¼ cup (20 g) moist coconut flakes
1¼ cups (310 ml) milk (nut or dairy)
1 cup (250 g) Greek yoghurt
½ pink lady apple, grated
½ green pear, grated
2 tbsp sultanas
1 tbsp chia seeds
1 tsp vanilla extract
½ tsp cinnamon
fruit, seeds and chopped nuts, to serve

This is child's play – other than the grating, they can make this themselves! Combine all the ingredients in a large bowl and mix around, then cover or place in an airtight container and pop in the fridge.

Try to make it the night before so life is easier in the morning, but a couple of hours soaking will do the trick. And then it will last for up to three days in the fridge.

To serve, add whatever fresh fruit, seeds and nuts that you like. In our house, it's always a fruit face.

NOTE: *Bircher porridge will keep in the fridge for up to three days, so it's a great make-ahead breakfast.*

'Fruit faces help make this healthy breakfast fun for kids!'

BAKED ITALIAN EGGS

SERVES 2

160 g speck, cut into 1 cm-thick lardons
400 g can baby Roma tomatoes
1 fresh cayenne chilli, sliced
1 tbsp extra-virgin olive oil
¼ bunch oregano, roughly chopped
2 basil sprigs, roughly chopped
1 thyme sprig, roughly chopped
4 extra-large eggs
40 g taleggio, frozen, plus extra, to serve

Preheat the oven to 165°C and then get cracking on these eggs!

Put the speck in a round ovenproof dish and place in the oven to render slowly while you cook the tomatoes. My ideal dish is 24 cm diameter, but you could go slightly smaller or larger if that's all you have.

Empty the can of tomatoes into a bowl and use your fingers to burst them (an apron will be your friend here) squeezing out their juice. Pour into a small saucepan and place over medium heat. Bring to a simmer and cook until thick and reduced, which will take about 10–15 minutes.

Once the speck is rendered and beginning to caramelise, add the chilli and bake until the chilli is softened and the speck is crispy. The smell now is amazing.

Stir the olive oil into the tomato mixture and season with salt and pepper, then add it to the speck and chilli. Keep in mind that the speck will be salty so don't over do the seasoning. Fold through the herbs, reserving a few basil leaves for garnish.

Make four divots in the sauce for the eggs, crack the eggs in and season with a touch of salt. (Alternatively, you can divide the sauce into two cast-iron skillets and add two eggs to each.) Coarsely grate the taleggio and sprinkle it over, then use a spoon to tuck some of the cheese under the sauce.

Bake until the egg whites are set but the yolks are still runny, probably about 10 minutes, then finish with another light sprinkle of taleggio and a few torn basil leaves. These come up volcanic hot so let them rest for at least 5 minutes before serving up.

'There are a million egg dishes out there, but trust me, there's nothing better than waking up to this one!'

BREAKFAST TORTILLAS

MAKES 6 TORTILLAS

FOR THE TORTILLAS

| 30 g rendered beef fat |
| 125 g hot water |
| 100 g yellow masa harina |
| 4 g salt |

FOR THE GUACAMOLE

| 1 avocado |
| ½ lime, juiced |
| 30 g extra-virgin olive oil |
| salt to taste |

FOR THE SALSA

| 2 roma tomatoes |
| ½ red onion, diced |
| ¼ bunch coriander, roughly chopped |
| ½ lime, juiced |
| salt to taste |

THE REST

| firm chorizo, diced |
| 2 eggs |
| feta cheese, crumbled |
| jalapeño hot sauce |

TO SERVE

| grapeseed oil |
| 1 chorizo sausage, diced |
| 2 eggs |
| guacamole |
| pickled jalapeños |
| cheddar or Monterey Jack cheese, grated |

To make the tortillas, in a bowl combine the beef fat with the hot water and stir into the masa flour. Season with salt to taste, be heavy handed. In the bowl, work it into a ball then put on the bench and knead until very smooth.

Divide the dough into six 30 g portions and press with a tortilla press or place between two sheets of baking paper and slowly and evenly press down with a baking dish until the dough is a thin disc. You don't want any cracks in them. If you do then put back into a ball and press again.

Get your cast-iron pan over high heat, and when it's super hot cook the tortillas one at a time for 1 minute each side. The beef fat keeps the pan non-stick so you don't need to add any oil before you cook the tortillas. As each one is cooked, place on a flat teatowel and fold over so they remain warm.

Put your diced up chorizo in a pan and fry up with a little bit of oil. I like mine super crispy but you make that call. As you're part way through cooking, push the chorizo to one side of the pan and crack two eggs into the other side so they are cooking in the chorizo fat. Delicious. Gently break the yolks and then stir through the whole pan so the chorizo and eggs are combined.

While this is cooking, put all your guacamole ingredients in a bowl and mash with a fork. That was easy. Then put all the salsa ingredients in a bowl and season to taste. I like to use white pepper but you can just go with salt and/or pepper.

Then it's time to build your tortilla – eggs, salsa, guacamole and feta cheese. Then if your little heart desires, add on some jalapeno hot sauce for a spicy kick.

'I'm told this isn't a healthy breakfast choice. Pfft.'

BREAKFAST CLASSICS

GLASGOW ROLLS

SERVES 6

270 ml tepid water

7 g sachet fast-acting instant yeast

1½ tsp caster sugar

2¾ cup (425 g) strong bread flour

2 tsp sea salt flakes

2 tsp sunflower oil

¼ cup (50 g) rice flour, for dusting

NOTE: *After shaping the rolls, they can be placed in the fridge or frozen to prove and bake later.*

Being able to make these rolls will change your life. To make the rolls, pour 170 ml of the water into a small bowl, add the yeast and whisk in. Then add the sugar and whisk again, then set aside to activate.

In a large bowl, combine the flour and salt, then drizzle the oil over. Use your hands to work the oil into the flour, creating a breadcrumb consistency. Use a rubber spatula to make a well in the centre of the flour then add the yeast mixture and remaining 100 ml of water. Use the spatula to mix, working the water into the flour.

When it comes together into a rough ball, turn the dough out onto a clean work surface and knead the dough for 10 minutes (you can use a stand mixer with a hook attachment on medium speed if you prefer) until it's smooth and elastic. Form the dough into a smooth ball then dust the work surface with rice flour and gently coat the dough in rice flour.

Lightly spray the bowl with oil and place the dough inside, then cover with a clean damp tea towel or plastic bag and set aside to prove for 1–1½ hours. You'll know this is done when they have doubled in size.

Dust the work bench with rice flour and turn the dough out onto the floured surface. Then you want to make them into flat discs so firmly tap the dough all over to remove the air pockets. Roll the flattened dough tightly into a log shape and use a knife or pastry scraper to cut the log into six 110 g pieces. Dust with rice flour and use your hand to flatten them slightly. Leave covered on the bench for 5 minutes, then pat them down again, sprinkle with rice flour and place them about 1 cm apart on a baking tray lined with baking paper. Sprinkle with rice flour and then cover with a damp tea towel, plastic bag or a plastic container and leave for 1–1½ hours until doubled in size again.

Meanwhile, preheat the oven to 250°C and place a small, heatproof bowl on the bottom rack.

When the dough has risen, add 2–3 ice cubes to the hot bowl at the bottom of the oven. Weird but necessary for humidity. Then place the bread rolls on a rack above the bowl and bake for 10 minutes until golden brown. For well-fired (darker) rolls, bake for 12 minutes.

When it's finally time to serve, butter the rolls and add tomato sauce and HP Sauce. We call this 'tartan sauce'. Then start building the roll of your dreams with a slice of square sausage, a tattie scone and a fried egg. Boom!

SQUARE SAUSAGE

SERVES 6

- 700 g pork mince
- 300 g beef mince
- 250 g fatty pork belly, minced
- 1¼ cups (150 g) dried breadcrumbs
- 1 tsp ground nutmeg
- 1 tsp ground mace (or extra nutmeg)
- 2 tsp ground coriander
- 2½ tsp salt flakes
- 1 tsp black pepper
- 1 tsp white pepper
- ½ cup (125 ml) chilled water
- grapeseed oil, for frying

Line a loaf tin with cling film (unless you are using a silicone loaf tin).

Combine the minces in a large mixing bowl and add the breadcrumbs. Wearing a pair of gloves if you like, use your hands to work the breadcrumbs through the mince.

Combine the spices, salt and peppers with the chilled water in a bowl and whisk. Pour into the mince mixture and massage it in, squeezing the spices through the mince until well incorporated.

Bring the mince mixture into a ball and compact it to remove any air pockets. Shape into a log to fit your loaf tin. Press the mince firmly into the tin and smooth the surface. Cover and refrigerate for 2 hours or overnight.

To cook, cut the sausage into 1.5 cm-thick slices. Heat a little grapeseed oil in a large frying pan over medium heat and add 2–3 slices of sausage. Cook the sausage until dark golden brown (about 3 minutes each side). Repeat for 6 serves.

'A Scottish fry-up essential! My serving suggestion: Glasgow roll, square sausage, fried eggs, bacon and tartan sauce (that's HP Sauce plus Heinz Tomato Ketchup). You'll find yer Scottish accent may just get a wee bit thicker.'

TATTIE SCONES

SERVES 6

2–3 medium potatoes (Dutch cream is best!), peeled and chopped

60 g unsalted butter, chopped

¾ cup (120 g) plain flour

Cook the potatoes in salted boiling water until soft, then strain and leave in the colander until cooled.

Pop the potatoes in a large mixing bowl and add the butter, then mash until smooth, season with salt and pepper.

Fold in the flour to the potatoes and form the mixture into a ball, taking care not to overwork the dough. Then divide into two balls.

Lightly flour your bench and roll out each ball of dough to between 5–7.5 mm thick and use a wooden skewer to press two lines into the dough like a big cross, creating quarters.

Heat a lightly greased frying pan over medium heat and cook for about 3 minutes each side until golden brown. Serve hot, and better still with a square sausage!

SCRAMBLED EGGS
WITH 'NDUJA AND LEFTOVER PIZZA DOUGH

SERVES 1

leftover raw pizza dough (a handful is enough)
2 eggs
1 tbsp 'nduja (spicy, spreadable salami)
shaved Parmigiano Reggiano, to serve

Preheat a pizza oven to 400°C or a conventional oven to 250°C.

Press your leftover pizza dough into a small circle, about the size of your outstretched hand. Bake in a pizza oven for 2–3 minutes or in a conventional oven for about 10 minutes.

Meanwhile, in a bowl, gently whisk the eggs with a fork. I never use a whisk.

Place a non-stick frying pan over low heat and cook the 'nduja gently until it's warm and a small amount of the fat has begun to render. Add the eggs and cook, stirring constantly and gently. When the egg is done it will have a velvety, smooth texture without any large curds. This should take about 5 minutes of continual stirring over low heat.

Season with salt and serve immediately with the pizza, garnished with shaved parmesan and freshly cracked black pepper. If you can't handle heat then go easy on the 'nduja.

'I don't get hangovers, but if I did this would be my breakfast choice.'

CHORIZO CORN FRITTERS
WITH EGGS AND AVOCADO SALSA

SERVES 2

100 g chorizo, diced

2 eggs

2 tbsp potato flour

2 tbsp cornflour

2 tbsp plain flour

1 tsp baking powder

⅓ cup (80 ml) milk

1 tsp grated garlic

1 tsp grated fresh ginger

¾ cup (150 g) fresh corn kernels

1 spring onion, sliced

zest of 1 lime

FOR THE SALSA

1 avocado, diced

juice of 1 lime

2 dashes jalapeño hot sauce

¼ bunch coriander, finely chopped

extra-virgin olive oil, to drizzle

Heat a splash of oil in a frying pan over high heat and fry the chorizo for 2 minutes. Lower heat and remove the chorizo, leaving the oil in the pan. Crack the eggs into the pan and fry gently over low heat until cooked to your liking. Remove the eggs and set aside but don't wash this pan as you'll need it (and the chorizo oil) later.

Meanwhile, to make the fritter batter, whisk together the flours, baking powder, milk, garlic and ginger until smooth, then set aside.

To make the salsa, place the avocado in a bowl with the lime juice, jalapeño hot sauce and coriander. Season to taste with salt, add a drizzle of extra-virgin olive oil, and carefully mix without mushing. Pop that to the side.

Add the chorizo, corn, spring onion, lime zest and a pinch of salt to the fritter batter and mix well. Place the chorizo pan back over medium–high heat and when the oil is hot use a large spoon to drop four blobs of batter into the pan about 2 cm apart. Cook for 2–3 minutes, until golden brown and crispy, on each side.

To serve, place two corn fritters in the centre of each plate, gently lay a fried egg on top and put as much avocado salsa as you can on top.

CAMPARI-CURED GRAVLAX
WITH LEMON COTTAGE CHEESE SAUCE
SERVES 12

4 tsp fennel seeds
4 tsp coriander seeds
3 tsp white peppercorns
700 g flaked salt
1 cup (230 g) caster sugar
zest of 4 blood oranges
zest of 1 lemon
150 ml Campari
1.3 kg side of salmon, skin on
2½ tbsp horseradish paste
10 g lemon verbena, finely chopped
1 bunch lemon balm, finely chopped
½ bunch fennel fronds, finely chopped
½ bunch flat-leaf parsley, finely chopped

FOR THE LEMON COTTAGE CHEESE SAUCE

500 g cottage cheese
juice of 3 lemons
1¼ tbsp white soy sauce

In a dry frying pan over medium heat, toast the fennel seeds, coriander seeds and white peppercorns until aromatic, then put into a mortar and pestle and crush.

Combine the crushed spices in a bowl with the salt, sugar and citrus zest and mix well, using your hands to distribute spices and zests thoroughly through the salt and sugar. Pour in the Campari and mix well.

Lightly score the skin of the salmon. On a large tray (it needs to be slightly larger than the salmon), spread half of the curing salt mixture then place the salmon skin-side down on top of it, then cover with the remaining salt mixture, making sure to coat the sides.

Cover with cling film and place a weight on top, then put it in the fridge to cure for 24 hours, turning the fish after 12 hours. To turn the fish, uncover it, scrape off the top layer of curing salt, turn it over and cover with salt again, then wrap and weight as before.

After 24 hours, remove the surplus curing salt from the salmon, wash the salmon and thoroughly pat dry. Brush the flesh side only with a thin layer of horseradish, then cover with the lemon verbena, lemon balm, fennel fronds and parsley. Wrap the salmon in cling film, then place herb-side down on a tray. Cover with the weight again and leave for another 1–2 hours to allow the herbs to adhere to the fish.

To make the lemon cottage cheese sauce, place all ingredients in a blender and blitz until smooth. Super tasty, super simple.

Cutting the salmon is important so grab a long sharp knife so you can slice it as thinly as possible. Place skin side down, cut through, and as you hit the skin use your knife to scrape it off the skin. Repeat.

If serving individual portions, spoon 2½ tablespoons of the cottage cheese sauce into the centre of each serving plate and spread with the back of a spoon. I pat the underside of the plate so it spreads without any marks but that might be a bit over the top. Then arrange the salmon on top of the sauce. If you're serving on a platter, spread half of the cottage cheese sauce on the bottom of the platter and the rest in a serving bowl, then arrange the whole sliced salmon on top.

Jock on Nyul Nyul Country in the Dampier Peninsula, the Kimberley, Western Australia, in April 2019.
Credit: Luke Eblen

'At night, we'd cook in this makeshift bush kitchen in the middle of the camp, built of timber and corrugated iron and lit by the flickering flames of cooking fires and portable lamps. Overhead, lightning would crack through the sky as the humidity threatened to break into torrential rain.

Those nights were the first time in a long, long period that I felt at peace. I'll always be grateful to Bruno Dann and his family for allowing me to share that time with them.'

GREEN BREAKFAST SALAD
WITH FARRO AND TAHINI VERDE

SERVES 1

- 30 g kale, chopped (stalks removed)
- 50 g snow peas, thinly sliced on a diagonal
- 1 cup (100 g) cooked farro
- 80 g streaky bacon, diced and pan-fried
- ½ avocado, roughly diced
- 2 soft-poached eggs
- 2 tbsp smoked almonds, roughly chopped
- 1 tbsp sunflower seeds, toasted
- extra-virgin olive oil, to drizzle
- 1 lime cheek, to serve

FOR THE TAHINI VERDE DRESSING

- ½ cup (130 g) tahini
- ½ bunch mint leaves (about 30 g)
- 1 small bunch parsley leaves (about 30 g)
- ⅓ cup (85 ml) extra-virgin olive oil
- 1 tbsp jalapeño hot sauce
- 200 ml lime juice
- 2½ tbsp water

To make the tahini verde dressing, place all the ingredients in a blender and blitz until smooth. Easy.

Then combine the kale, snow peas, farro, bacon and avocado in a large bowl and coat with a quarter of the dressing. Season with salt and pepper. Place this mix onto a plate and top with the poached eggs. Sprinkle with the smoked almonds and sunflower seeds, drizzle with some extra-virgin olive oil, and place a lime cheek on the side.

There's enough dressing for four serves, but if you don't use it all then pop it in the fridge. It will keep for a couple of weeks.

CHILLI COFFEE EGGS

SERVES 2

50 g butter
1 tsp nasi lemak sambal
1 tsp chilli jam
1 tsp crispy chilli oil
1 tsp Tabasco
small handful coriander leaves, plus extra to garnish
1 lime, quartered
4 eggs
1 avocado, halved
2 slices sourdough, toasted
1 shot espresso

This will blow your mind. Melt the butter in a pan over medium heat, then add the sambal, chilli jam, crispy chilli oil and Tabasco, and stir it all together. Gently season then add the coriander and a squeeze of lime juice and give the pan a shoogle. Crack the eggs into the chilli mixture, spacing them evenly around the pan.

While the eggs are cooking, prep the avocado. Scoop out each half and thinly slice, fanning out the slices to fit a piece of sourdough and place on top of the toast.

When the eggs are about halfway cooked, pour the espresso shot over the chilli mix around the eggs and give the pan another shoogle.

When the egg whites are firm and a little crispy around the edges and the yolks are still runny, they're ready. Lift out the eggs and place two on each avocado-loaded slice of sourdough toast. Garnish with extra coriander, the remaining chilli mixture and an extra squeeze of lime and you're ready to go.

'I was just mucking around the first time I tried this, but with the bitterness of the coffee up against the chilli, it was just too good not to have again and again.'

BREAKFAST CLASSICS

GRILLED STONE FRUIT
WITH WAFFLES AND SALTED BUTTERSCOTCH SAUCE

SERVES 2

3 (about 500 g) ripe but firm peaches

3 (about 160 g) ripe but firm apricots

4 store-bought waffles

FOR THE SALTED BUTTERSCOTCH SAUCE

80 g unsalted butter

1 cup (190 g) brown sugar

2 tsp salt

150 ml cream

To make the butterscotch sauce, place the butter, sugar, salt and cream in a small saucepan over medium–high heat. Bring to the boil and simmer for 2 minutes. Keep an eye on this – you don't want it going too dark or having a close-to-burnt taste. Remove from the heat and pour into a sauceboat or jug. This is a recipe you need up your sleeve or in your fridge at all times.

Heat a griddle pan over high heat. Halve your peaches and apricots and remove the pits. You need to decide how big you want to cut your fruit, just keep them thick enough not to get mushy when they're cooked – I would get 6 slices from a peach and 2 from an apricot. Place the fruit on the hot griddle and char on all sides, then place in a bowl and set aside.

This is the express/easy version so toast the waffles in a toaster or hot oven as per the packet instructions. Divide the waffles between two plates and cascade the grilled stone fruit over the top and drizzle liberally with butterscotch sauce. Serve immediately. This wonder goes well with a dollop of plain yoghurt and a few mint leaves but I'll leave that up to you to play with.

'Use whatever stone fruit is in season at the time for this dish. My preference is peaches, plums, nectarines and apricots.'

FLUFFY COCONUT PANCAKES
WITH MANGO SALSA

SERVES 4

¾ cup (100 g) plain flour

½ cup (60 g) coconut flour

1 tbsp jaggery, grated (see Note)

2 tsp baking powder

1 tsp salt

1 egg, lightly beaten

1½ cups (375 ml) milk

50 g unsalted butter, melted and cooled

1 tsp vanilla paste

1 banana (about 150 g), diced

1⅓ cups (120 g) moist coconut flakes

butter or grapeseed oil, for greasing

FOR THE MANGO SALSA

1½ tbsp jaggery, grated

zest and juice of 1 lime

2½ tbsp ginger, minced

2 mangoes, diced

2 oranges, segmented

2 tbsp black sesame seeds

¼ cup (20 g) toasted coconut flakes

To make the mango salsa, combine the jaggery, lime juice, zest and ginger. Add the remaining ingredients and combine. Let stand while you make your pancakes to allow the flavours to merge.

For the pancakes, whisk together the flours, jaggery, baking powder and salt in a large mixing bowl. I use my stick blender, so if you have one use that.

Combine the egg, milk, butter and vanilla in a separate bowl and beat with a fork. Add the banana and coconut, then fold this mixture into the dry mixture, being careful not to overwork it.

Grease a non-stick frying pan with butter or oil then heat over medium heat.

When the pan is hot, add about a quarter of the pancake mix and cook for 3 minutes or until the surface begins to bubble. Carefully flip the pancake and cook for an additional 3 minutes. Repeat with remaining pancake mixture.

Serve the pancakes with the mango salsa on top.

NOTE: *Jaggery is an unrefined sugar, often sold in solid chunks that can be grated or crumbled into your dish. It gives an interesting, delicious flavour, but if you can't find jaggery, try brown sugar instead.*

Credit: Lauren Zonfrillo

'They're fluffy, and with mango, coconut and banana, they're seriously tropical. These pancakes can be for brekky, dessert, or a sneaky snack!'

CREPES
WITH SALTED BUTTERSCOTCH SAUCE

SERVES 4

FOR THE CREPES

1⅓ cups (330 ml) milk

¾ cup (115 g) plain flour

3 tsp sugar

1 tsp salt

3 eggs

2 tsp grapeseed oil

butter, for greasing

FOR THE SALTED BUTTERSCOTCH SAUCE

80 g unsalted butter

1 cup (190 g) brown sugar

2 tsp salt

150 ml cream

Place all crepe ingredients except the butter in a large bowl and whisk into a smooth, thin batter. I use a stick blender to make sure it's super smooth. Let it sit for a bit if you have the time.

Next make the butterscotch sauce. Place the butter, sugar, salt and cream in a small saucepan over medium–high heat. Bring to the boil and simmer for 2 minutes. Keep an eye on this – you don't want it going too dark or having a close-to-burnt taste. Remove from heat and pour into a sauceboat or jug.

Lightly grease your crepe pan – to do this, put in some butter then rub it around with a folded-up piece of paper towel so there's only a tiny amount on the pan. You can then reuse the paper towel to regrease the pan after each crepe.

Heat the pan over medium–high heat. When the pan is hot, pour in just enough batter to coat the bottom of your crepe pan and move the pan around to spread the mixture evenly. Let it cook for about 45 seconds each side. To flip the crepe, use a wooden skewer to pull down the edge of the crepe from the pan and then flip it. Take care not to overcook them; crepes are meant to be blond with a slight brown colour, not crispy.

Once cooked, place the crepe over an inverted plate so it hangs down the sides. Repeat with the remaining batter and layer up the crepes over the plate until you're ready to serve.

NOTE: *These crepes reheat well, so if you need to, cover them in cling film and microwave on low for 30 seconds.*

'Make a massive batch of the sauce and store it in squeezy bottles in the fridge, then give it a quick zap in the microwave and it's good to go!'

'Papa and husband are my two favourite jobs. I've learnt through many mistakes that time with my family is the most precious gift.'

Jock napping at home in the Adelaide Hills with six-week-old Alfie, in April 2018.
Credit: Lauren Zonfrillo

Jock's REGULARS

AVA'S VEGAN BURGER

SERVES 4

400 g beetroot, peeled

330 g broccoli

500 g sweet potato

50 g shiitake mushrooms

250 g carrots, peeled

1¼ cups (200 g) pumpkin seeds

50 g mushroom oyster sauce

extra-virgin olive oil, to grill

4-6 slices vegan cheese

TO BUILD THE BURGERS

4 burger buns

tomato sauce, to serve

red onion, sliced into rounds and soaked in lemon juice

pickles, to serve

baby gem lettuce leaves, to serve

This is a vegan recipe, so let's get prepping on the veggies. Peel and chop the beetroot, sweet potato and carrots. Trim the broccoli and give the mushrooms a rough chop too. You want chunks around 1–2 cm, nothing too fine. Blanch everything in salted boiling water until just tender, then spread the lot out on trays lined with baking paper.

You need to dry them out so pop them in a dehydrator at 70°C for 2–3 hours, or if you're using a regular oven, set it to 50°C and leave them overnight. You're aiming for veggies that are just a little tacky, not bone-dry.

Next, get your blender out and blitz the pumpkin seeds with ¼ cup of water until they form a smooth butter. This is your binding magic – you won't need all of it, so set some aside for later.

Once your veggies are dry, run them through a coarse mincer or give them a few pulses in a food processor. You want texture not mush.

In a big bowl, mix the veggie mince with about 100 g of the pumpkin seed butter and the mushroom oyster sauce. Season well with salt and pepper. The mixture should hold together like a burger patty when pressed. If it's falling apart, add a bit more of the seed butter.

Now form the mix into four patties. Gloves are your friend here – beetroot stains like nobody's business. Press them firmly and evenly so they hold their shape.

Heat a grill or barbecue to 275°C. Place the patties on a wire rack set over a tray (or straight on the grill), brush with olive oil, and cook until golden, which will take about 5–8 minutes. When they're nearly done, top each with a couple of slices of vegan cheese and let it melt.

While the patties are cooking, toast your burger buns under the grill. Spread some of that leftover pumpkin seed butter on the bottom halves and tomato sauce on the tops.

Now build your burger: patty, pickles, red onion (soaked in lemon juice if you've got time), and baby gem lettuce. Pop the lid on and dig in.

'This is a burger that my daughter Ava and I made together. It's surprisingly easy and delicious – even for the non-vegans among us.'

MORTADELLA SANDWICH
WITH OLIVE BATH

SERVES 2

- 400 g mortadella, thinly sliced
- 1 tsp grapeseed oil
- 12 large, high-quality brined green olives, pitted and finely chopped
- 3 tbsp olive brine
- 3 tbsp red wine vinegar
- 1 tbsp extra-virgin olive oil
- 1 big pinch roughly chopped flat-leaf parsley
- 120 g spreadable cream cheese
- squeeze of lemon juice
- pinch of salt
- pinch of pepper
- 4 slices white sandwich bread

Loosely bunch up the mortadella into two piles that are about the size of your bread slices. Heat a splash of grapeseed oil in a non-stick frying pan over high heat. When the pan is hot and starting to smoke, sear the mortadella on both sides until golden and just starting to crisp up on the edges. Set aside.

Finely chop the olives and pop them in a small bowl. Add the olive brine, red wine vinegar, olive oil and parsley. Give it a stir and let it sit so the flavours can come together. My youngest daughter Isla drinks this if I'm not watching!

In a separate bowl, mix the cream cheese with lemon juice, a pinch of salt and some cracked pepper.

Spread the cream cheese mixture generously onto all the bread slices. Sandwich the mortadella in between and gently press together.

Use a very sharp knife to trim the crusts – light touch here so you don't squash the bread. Slice into fingers and serve with the olive bath on the side for dipping. I've never met anyone who doesn't love these.

'This is God's gift to sandwiches.'

SWORDFISH POLPETTE SPAGHETTI

SERVES 2

200 g dried spaghetti
1¾ tbsp extra-virgin olive oil
400 g can diced tomatoes

FOR THE POLPETTE

250 g swordfish, diced into 1 cm cubes
1 small garlic clove, minced
zest of 1 lemon
¼ cup (50 g) dried breadcrumbs
1 tbsp hazelnuts, roasted and finely chopped
2½ tbsp pitted green olives, sliced (reserve ½ tbsp for the sauce)
1½ tbsp capers, roughly chopped (reserve ½ tbsp for the sauce)
handful flat-leaf parsley, chopped (reserve half for the sauce)
2 eggs

Combine all the polpette ingredients in a large bowl – swordfish, garlic, lemon zest, breadcrumbs, hazelnuts, olives, capers, parsley and eggs – and season well with salt and pepper. Mix gently until combined, then roll into eight golf ball-sized meatballs, about 50 g each. I get the kids to do this bit. Pop them in the fridge to firm up for about an hour.

When you're ready to cook, bring a big pot of salted water to the boil and cook your spaghetti for 3 minutes less than what the packet says. Drain, but make sure to catch a good splash of that pasta water into a mug – you'll need it later.

In a wide frying pan, heat the olive oil over medium. Brown the polpette on all sides – about 30 seconds per side will do it – then add the reserved olives, capers and parsley. Give it all a toss, then pour in the diced tomatoes and bring to a simmer. Let it bubble gently for 15 minutes so the polpette cook through and the sauce thickens.

Add your spaghetti to the pan and toss to coat. Use some of the reserved pasta water to loosen the sauce if needed – you want it silky, not stodgy.

Plate it up, then add a final spoonful of sauce over the top from the pan.

'This dish makes an impressive yet super-simple dinner for two. It's light on garlic and all the other anti-lover fragrances, and it will be on the table in no time. Trust me, Italians know the language of love!'

JOCK'S REGULARS

PASTA E FAGIOLI CON CAVOLO NERO

SERVES 4

FOR THE STOCK

300 g dried borlotti beans, soaked overnight

1 parmesan rind (about 100 g), plus shaved parmesan, to serve

1 pancetta rind (about 100 g)

2 medium carrots, cut into 5 cm pieces

2 celery stalks, cut into 5 cm pieces

1 garlic bulb, halved crosswise

6 flat-leaf parsley sprigs

6 sage leaves

1 rosemary sprig

2 bay leaves

1 dried chilli

2 litres (8 cups) water

FOR THE SOUP

3 tbsp (60 ml) extra-virgin olive oil, plus extra, to serve

100 g lardo (pork fat), finely diced

1 smoked dried chilli, chopped, plus extra, to serve (optional)

2 sage leaves

3 basil leaves

1 large onion, finely chopped

2 garlic cloves, finely chopped

400 g can whole peeled tomatoes

¾ cup (175 ml) dry white wine

100 g dried maltagliati or other short pasta, cooked according to packet instructions

½ young head cavolo nero, blanched in salted water then cooked over the fire, cut into 5 cm pieces

Make this on a day when you're not in a rush and just want to potter around the kitchen. Start with the stock. Throw everything into a pot – borlotti beans, parmesan rind, pancetta rind, carrots, celery, garlic, parsley, sage, rosemary, bay leaves, chilli and water. Bring to a boil and skim any froth off the top. Lower the heat, pop the lid on and simmer gently until the beans are tender – about an hour and a half. Top up with more water if it's looking low.

Once the beans are done, season with salt and pepper and let the stock sit for 30 minutes. Scoop out and discard the veggies, rinds and herbs. Take about a third of the beans and blitz them with a splash of the stock, then pour that back into the pot to thicken things up a bit.

Now for the soup. In a separate pot, heat the olive oil over medium. Add the lardo and cook slowly until it starts to melt. Toss in the smoked chilli, sage, basil, onion and garlic. Let it all soften, give it 8 to 10 minutes.

Next, crush the tinned tomatoes with your hands and add them to the pot. Cook until it's reduced right down, then pour in the white wine. Let it bubble away until it's nearly gone, then add the beans and stock.

Let it all come together for about 10–15 minutes. Add your cooked pasta and the blanched cavolo nero. Stir it through and check the seasoning.

Serve it hot, with a generous drizzle of olive oil, a shower of parmesan and more chilli if you fancy a kick. This gets better and better as leftovers so make more than you need.

'While it's fair to say there are as many recipes for pasta e fagioli (pasta and beans) as there are Italian chefs, this recipe is special, at least to my family.

This recipe was translated from a very old Italian kitchen notebook that belonged to my Nonna Mallozzi and while the ingredients written within it may be simple, the dishes they make represent a time-honoured tradition that runs deep in my blood.'

JOCK'S REGULARS

SPAGHETTI CARBONARA

SERVES 2

250 g dried spaghetti
80 g guanciale (Italian cured pork), diced
1 egg
3 egg yolks
¾ cup (60 g) finely grated Pecorino Romano
¾ cup (60 g) finely grated Parmigiano Reggiano

Bring a pot of salted water to the boil and cook the spaghetti for 3 minutes less than the packet says. You want it properly al dente, it will finish cooking in the sauce.

While that's going, get your guanciale into a cold pan and place it over medium–high heat. Let the fat slowly render out as the pan heats, stirring often until it's golden and crispy. Scoop the guanciale into a bowl with paper towel to drain it and leave the fat in the pan – that's liquid gold. I like to season the fat with plenty of pepper at this stage.

In a separate bowl, whisk together the whole egg, the yolks, Pecorino and Parmigiano. Set it aside.

When the pasta's ready, drain it but keep a mugful of the pasta water.

Have the guanciale fat pan on a low heat, then add the hot pasta into the pan and stir so it's all coated.

Add about half the mug of pasta water into the egg and cheese mix and whisk well. Take the pan off the heat and pour in the egg and cheese mixture. Stir like mad, adding splashes of the reserved pasta water a bit at a time until the sauce goes glossy and coats every strand. It should cling, not pool. Then add the cooked guanciale and stir in.

Taste for seasoning – you probably won't need salt thanks to the guanciale, but an extra crack of pepper won't hurt. Cover with a clean tea towel and let it rest for a couple of minutes to finish thickening. When you're ready to serve, you can adjust the consistency with a bit more pasta water, then serve immediately.

'When I take a bite of spaghetti alla carbonara on a miserable day, I'm immediately back in my nonno's kitchen. Nonno cooked carbonara the way my dad did, and the way I do – properly. Guanciale, pecorino, parmigiano, eggs; that's it. No white wine, no onion, no garlic, no cream.

If you put cream in the sauce, you would not only disappoint my nonno, but ruin what is one of the greatest dishes in the world, elegant in its simplicity and heritage.

Please, I beg you, don't put cream in your fucking pasta carbonara.'

JOCK'S REGULARS

Jock's daily stop at Andrea Pansa in Amalfi, Italy, in July 2018.
Credit: Lauren Zonfrillo

'The world continues to adopt Italian traits. Whether it's in food or coffee — Italian never goes out of fashion.'

MAC 'N COTTAGE CHEESE

SERVES 2

2½ tsp smoked salt
200 g dried mezzi rigatoni
2 tsp grapeseed oil (optional)
300 g smoked speck, cut into lardons (optional)
400 g cottage cheese
4 egg yolks
4 tsp hickory spice rub
pinch of white pepper

Bring a pot of water to the boil with 2 teaspoons of the smoked salt, and cook the pasta until just al dente.

If you're using speck, heat a splash of grapeseed oil in a pan over medium heat and fry until golden and caramelised. Scoop it out with a slotted spoon and set aside on paper towel, but keep that rendered fat in the pan – you'll want that later.

Blend half the cottage cheese until smooth, then whisk it together with the remaining cottage cheese, egg yolks, hickory spice, up to ½ teaspoon of smoked salt and a pinch of white pepper.

Pour this mix into a pan (use the one with the speck fat if you're using it) and stir over medium heat until it just starts to simmer. Don't walk away, you don't want it to split. Once it's come together, take it off the heat.

Add your cooked pasta and speck (if using), and give everything a good stir to coat. Add a splash or two of the reserved pasta water if it needs loosening, you want it silky, not stodgy.

Cover the pan with a clean tea towel and let it sit for a couple of minutes to thicken slightly, then serve straight away. It's cheesy, smoky, a little bit fancy – and no one will know it's cottage cheese unless you tell them.

'Cottage cheese is my favourite hack for a quick mac and cheese that's simple to make and healthier than the regular version – and no one will notice the difference.'

JOCK'S REGULARS

'SCOTTISH' PIE

SERVES 8

½ tsp bicarbonate of soda

½ tsp salt

2 tbsp water

3½ tbsp grapeseed oil

1 kg beef mince

6 small to medium potatoes, peeled

1 tbsp grapeseed oil

2 onions, finely diced

3–4 medium carrots, finely diced

400 g portobello mushrooms, finely diced

5–6 garlic cloves, minced

2 tsp chopped thyme

2 tsp chopped rosemary

1 tsp smoked paprika

1 tsp sweet paprika

¼ cup (80 g) triple-concentrate tomato paste

1 cup (250 ml) red wine

6 bay leaves

400 ml red wine jus

400 ml gravy

5 tbsp HP Sauce

2 tbsp Worcestershire sauce

melted butter, for brushing

Preheat the oven to 250°C and grease a big baking dish.

In a bowl, mix the bicarb, salt, water and 2½ tablespoons of grapeseed oil. Add the beef mince and give it all a good toss – this helps tenderise the meat.

In a large frying pan over medium–high heat, fry the mince in batches. Don't crowd the pan – you want proper colour. Get it dark and caramelised, then scoop it out with a slotted spoon and set aside.

Pop your potatoes into a pot of cold salted water and bring to a simmer. Cook until they're just tender – they'll finish in the oven. Drain and let them cool a bit, then slice thickly.

Wipe out the pan, add a tablespoon of oil and cook the onion until golden. Then add the carrots, mushrooms, garlic, herbs and spices. Cook it all down until the pan's dry and everything's softened and smelling incredible.

Add the tomato paste, cook for a minute or two, then pour in the red wine. Let that bubble away and reduce by half. Now stir the cooked mince back in along with the bay leaves, red wine jus, gravy, HP sauce and Worcestershire sauce. Let it simmer for 15–20 minutes until thick and rich. Season to taste, then pick out the bay leaves.

Pour the mince mixture into your baking dish and layer the sliced potatoes neatly over the top. Brush generously with melted butter, season again with salt and pepper, and bake for 30–40 minutes until golden and bubbling.

This one's proper comfort food. Serve it hot, preferably with a nap afterwards.

'Sure, it's cottage pie. But we call it Scottish pie in our house.'

THE PERFECT STEAK

MAKES 1 STEAK

1 dry-aged rib-eye steak on the bone, at room temperature

grapeseed oil, for rubbing

red wine vinegar, a dash of water and a little shio koji (in a spray bottle)

2–3 rosemary sprigs

Let your rib-eye come to room temperature – cold steak + hot grill is not your friend. Season it generously with salt and pepper, and rub it with a little grapeseed oil.

Fire up your hibachi (or barbecue or grill pan if that's what you've got). If you've got cherry wood, toss a few chunks onto the coals to build that beautiful smoke.

Meanwhile, preheat your oven to 50°C, or use the 'keep warm' setting.

When the grill is blazing hot and smoking, place the steak on, starting with the sides to get some crust around the edges. Then grill the flat sides, turning every minute or so until the crust is rich and dark. You're aiming for an internal temp of 45°C – medium–rare perfection. If it's charring too quickly, spritz it with a mix of red wine vinegar, water and a splash of shio koji. That cools the surface and adds punch.

In the last minute of cooking, chuck a couple of rosemary sprigs onto the coals to infuse the smoke with that woody, herby hit. Once it's done, transfer the steak to the oven to rest. However long it took to cook, that's how long it needs to rest. No shortcuts.

To serve, remove the bone, slice the steak into thick, even strips, and scatter with a little more salt. Serve it up with the bone on the side, don't leave any meat on there.

'Caramelisation – rich, dark, mahogany, beautiful – that's what we're looking for.'

JOCK'S REGULARS

SOUTHERN FRIED CHICKEN

MAKES 10 PIECES

1 whole chicken, jointed into 10 pieces
475 g plain flour
1¼ cups (200 g) cornflour
1½ tsp baking powder
2 tsp salt, plus extra, to serve
vegetable oil, for deep-frying

FOR THE BUTTERMILK BRINE

600 ml buttermilk
2 large eggs
2 tsp salt
2¼ tbsp paprika
4 tbsp white pepper
1½ tbsp garlic powder
1½ tsp dried oregano
1 tsp cayenne pepper

Start this one a couple of days ahead for best results. First, air-dry the chicken in the fridge overnight, uncovered, on a wire rack. This step is key for getting that proper crunch later.

Next day, mix up your buttermilk brine: whisk together the buttermilk, eggs, salt, paprika, white pepper, garlic powder, oregano and cayenne. Place the chicken pieces in a big bowl or container, pour over the brine, and massage it into every crevice. Cover and marinate in the fridge overnight.

The next day, sift the plain flour, cornflour, baking powder and salt into a big bowl. Spoon 4–5 tablespoons of the buttermilk brine into the flour and rub it in with your fingers to form those craggy, crispy bits that cling to the edges of your chicken.

Roll each chicken piece in the flour mix, pressing firmly to coat every nook. Once they're all dusted, let them sit in the flour for 1–2 hours – this gives the coating time to really stick.

Heat your oil to 190°C in a deep fryer or a big, heavy pot – don't fill it more than halfway. When it's ready, gently lower in the chicken pieces (work in batches) and fry for 8–10 minutes or until they're golden, crisp and floating.

Drain the chicken on a wire rack and hit it with a final sprinkle of salt while it's still hot. Serve it fresh, loud, and with a stack of napkins. I also have some Bread and Butter Pickles with mine, you decide.

'Who needs the Colonel? Seriously. This fried chicken is delicious, shatteringly crunchy and stays juicy because of the buttermilk brine. Get some mates together and get frying.'

Jock after Restaurant Orana won the Restaurant of the Year at the 2019 Good Food Guide Awards, in Sydney, October 2018.
Credit: Kristoffer Paulsen

'Winning awards does feel fucking great. As the accolades and awards piled up, the thing we'd always wanted to happen began to manifest.

In the space of a few years, Orana went from begging critics to have a conversation with us about green ant sorbet to being considered the best restaurant in the country, and we were booked out for months on end by serious foodies who were travelling to Adelaide specifically to celebrate Indigenous food. And that was pretty amazing.'

BUTTER CHICKEN

SERVES 4

FOR THE CHICKEN TIKKA

8 boneless and skinless chicken thighs
1½ tbsp grated garlic
1½ tbsp grated ginger
½ tsp Kashmiri chilli powder
¾ tsp smoked paprika
2 tsp salt
juice of 2 lemons
300 g labneh
¾ tsp ground turmeric
½ tsp ground cumin
½ tsp ground coriander
½ tsp ground green cardamom
¼ tsp smoked paprika
1 tsp garam marsala
3 tsp grapeseed oil
100 g butter, melted, for basting

FOR THE BUTTER CHICKEN SAUCE

1½ tbsp grapeseed oil
1½ tbsp grated ginger
1½ tbsp grated garlic
¾ cup (200 g) triple-concentrate tomato paste
¾ tsp ground turmeric
½ tsp ground cumin
½ tsp ground coriander
½ tsp smoked paprika
2⅓ cups (600 ml) water
1½ tbsp jaggery (unrefined sugar), grated
2 tsp fenugreek leaves, roasted and ground
¼ cup (60 ml) cream
30 g unsalted butter

Start by cutting the chicken thighs into quarters. In a large bowl, whisk together the garlic, ginger, Kashmiri chilli, ½ tsp smoked paprika, salt and juice of one lemon. Add the chicken, give it a good mix, and let it marinate for 30 minutes.

Then whisk together the labneh, turmeric, cumin, coriander, cardamom, remaining smoked paprika, garam masala and grapeseed oil. Stir it through the chicken, cover and marinate in the fridge for at least an hour (longer if you've got time).

While the chicken is marinating, make the sauce. In a heavy-based pot over medium heat, heat the oil and sauté the ginger, garlic, tomato paste and spices with a pinch of salt. Stir often – you want the paste to deepen and the aromatics to shine.

Add the water, the rest of the grapeseed oil and more salt to taste. Bring to a boil, pop a lid on and simmer for 5 minutes. Then take the lid off and let it reduce for 15 minutes until thickened and rich.

Whisk in the jaggery and fenugreek. Simmer a few minutes more, then stir through the cream and finally the butter. Taste and adjust your seasoning – this is your base, so it's important you get it right.

Thread the marinated chicken onto metal skewers – 4 to 5 pieces per skewer – and grill over a hibachi or barbecue until charred at the edges and cooked through. Baste with melted butter in the last few minutes for that extra richness.

Once cooked, remove the chicken from the skewers and stir it into the sauce. Heat gently to combine then serve with homemade naan (opposite page) and rice.

NOTE: *If you don't have a hibachi you can use a barbecue or grill pan to give the chicken a smoky flavour.*

NAAN

MAKES 4

- 7 g sachet instant active dry yeast
- 1 tbsp sugar
- 150 ml warm water
- 2¼ cups (350 g) bread flour
- 3 tsp salt
- ¾ cup (180 g) plain yoghurt
- 1 tsp each nigella, coriander and mustard seeds
- 150 g unsalted butter

Start by activating your yeast. In a small bowl, mix the sachet of yeast with the sugar and warm water. Leave it for 5 minutes – it should get all bubbly and frothy.

Meanwhile, in a large mixing bowl, combine the bread flour and salt. Once the yeast is ready, pour it into the flour along with the yoghurt. Get your hands in there and bring it together into a shaggy dough, then tip it out onto a lightly floured bench and knead for about 5 minutes until it's smooth and elastic.

Grease a clean bowl with a little oil, pop the dough in, cover with cling film or a damp tea towel and let it rise in a warm spot for about 45–60 minutes, or until doubled in size.

While it's rising, toast the nigella seeds in a dry pan. Tip them into a bowl. Then add the coriander and mustard seeds to the same pan, reduce the heat, and add the butter. Let it melt, then bring it to a gentle simmer. Once the milk solids start to sink and darken, remove from the heat and strain to get a clear, spiced butter. Set aside.

Once the dough has doubled, tip it out onto a floured surface and divide it into four 150 g portions. Pat each one into a rough oval shape – no need to be perfect.

Heat a frying pan or skillet over high heat until it's smoking. Cook each naan for about 2 minutes per side – it should puff up and get charred in spots. Don't overcrowd the pan.

When they're hot off the pan, brush with your infused butter and sprinkle with the toasted nigella seeds. Serve straight away.

BLACK PEPPER MUD CRAB

SERVES 4

1 kg mud crab

vegetable oil, for deep frying

2 tbsp ghee

½ brown onion, diced

50 g ginger, roughly chopped

6 garlic cloves, roughly chopped

1 long red chilli, roughly chopped

½ lemongrass bulb, roughly chopped

2½ tbsp black peppercorns

1 tsp mountain peppercorns

1 tsp dried shrimp

2 cups (500 ml) chicken stock

2½ tbsp dark soy sauce

1 tbsp light soy sauce

30 g palm sugar, roughly chopped

1½ tbsp oyster sauce

25 g tamarind paste

25 g candlenuts, roughly chopped

20 g fermented soybeans

3 tsp liquid shio koji (natural flavour enhancer)

⅔ cup (140 g) potato flour

⅓ cup (50 g) tapioca flour

⅓ cup (50 g) rice flour

2 limes, halved

1 bunch coriander, roughly chopped

Let's get messy! Start by cleaning and portioning the crab – give it a good rinse and crack the claws and legs with the back of a knife. Set it aside.

Fill your fryer or a large pot with oil, no more than halfway, and heat the oil to 190°C. While that's warming, make the sauce base. In a large frying pan over medium heat, melt the ghee and add the onion, ginger, garlic, chilli and lemongrass. Let it all sweat down for about 20 minutes until soft and fragrant.

Meanwhile, blitz the black peppercorns, mountain pepper and dried shrimp in a blender or spice grinder until you've got a fine powder.

Add that spice mix to the pan, stir through and let it cook out for about a minute. Then pour in the chicken stock, both soy sauces, palm sugar, oyster sauce, tamarind, candlenuts and fermented soybeans. Let it bubble gently, stirring often, until it reduces to a thick, rich sauce, about 5 minutes. Season with shio koji to taste.

In a separate bowl, mix the potato, tapioca and rice flours. Toss the crab pieces in the flour mix, making sure they're well coated.

Working in batches, fry the crab for 2–3 minutes until lightly golden. Drain on paper towel. Once all the crab is fried, toss it into a big bowl with the black pepper sauce and coat everything generously.

To serve, pile the crab high on a platter, squeeze over fresh lime, and scatter with loads of chopped coriander. It's messy, it's spicy, it's unreal.

LIMONCELLO CHICKEN TRAYBAKE

SERVES 4

1.8 kg chicken
¼ cup limoncello
2 red onions
1 each red, yellow and green capsicums
4 garlic cloves
1 dried chilli, chopped
1 tbsp honey
1 tsp dijon mustard
2 tbsp extra-virgin olive oil
1 tbsp colotura (Italian fish sauce, can be substituted with Asian fish sauce)
1 tbsp red wine vinegar
1 kg small chat potatoes
3 lemons, halved
3 sprigs basil
400 g cherry tomatoes, on the vine

Preheat your oven to 200°C.

First, sort out the chicken. Pat it dry with kitchen paper and remove the wishbone if you're working with a whole bird – it makes portioning easier. Chop it into 8 pieces, or use marylands or drumsticks. Whatever works. Just make sure everything's roughly the same size so it cooks evenly.

Pop the chicken into a bowl with a couple of generous pinches of salt and the limoncello. Get your hands in there and give it a good mix. If you've got the time, let it sit for an hour – it will brine slightly and stay juicy. If not, 10 minutes will still do the job.

While the chicken's soaking up the good stuff, chop your onions into wedges and your capsicums into large, even chunks.

In a separate bowl, whisk together the garlic, dried chilli, honey, mustard, olive oil, colatura and red wine vinegar. This is your traybake magic.

Grab a large roasting tin. Scatter the potatoes over the base, followed by the onion, capsicum, and lemon halves. Nestle in the chicken pieces on top. Tuck the basil sprigs around the tray and drizzle everything with your honey-mustard dressing.

Bake for 20 minutes, then add the cherry tomatoes (leave them on the vine) and bake for another 20 minutes until the chicken is golden, sticky and cooked through.

Serve it straight from the tray. It's rustic, vibrant and impossible not to love.

'I made this in a rush one day in Puglia when our friends invited a heap of people over at the last minute. Conveniently, our friends made their own limoncello so there was plenty to go round.'

JOCK'S REGULARS

Snacks AND COCKTAILS

COCKTAIL GARNISHES

MAKES 3 LARGE JARS

1 blood orange

1–2 limes

1 pineapple, peeled

1 orange

1 apple

Preheat your oven to 60°C. If it doesn't go that low, you can set it to 90°C, just keep an eye on things.

Thinly slice all your fruit – blood orange, limes, pineapple, orange, and apple – into rounds. Try to keep them as uniform as you can so they dry evenly.

Lay them out in a single layer on lined baking trays. Don't let them overlap.

Bake at 60°C for 12 hours. If you're working with 90°C, bake for around 3 hours instead, turning the fruit halfway and watching closely so they don't colour too much.

Once dried and crisp, store them in airtight glass jars. They'll last up to a year if you keep them in a cool, dark place. Use them as snacks, in your cocktails, or on your cheese platters.

'Dehydrated fruit = snack AND cocktail garnish!'

APEROL SOUR

MAKES 1

Most people use half the amount of gin in this cocktail, but Jock was a bit heavy-handed! Feel free to use less if you prefer. You could also reduce the sugar syrup for a less sweet drink.

2 shots (60 ml) Aperol
1 shot (30 ml) gin
3 tsp (15 ml) lemon juice, plus up to 15 ml more to taste
2 tsp simple sugar syrup
1 small egg white
bitters, to finish

Combine all the ingredients, except the bitters, in a cocktail shaker without ice. Give this a violent shake so the egg whites are activated and do their thing. Then add a lot of ice, and shake again for the same amount of time. Taste and add more lemon juice if desired.

Strain into a chilled glass, and garnish with a few dashes of bitters.

VESPER MARTINI

MAKES 1

This became our drink of choice when we were living in Melbourne; we would drink them at Gimlet and Gerald's Bar. Most of our Vesper consumption was between these two places, but Jock would whip one up at home here and there.

¼ shot (7.5 ml) Cocchi Americano vermouth
scant shot (25 ml) vodka
1½ shots (45 ml) gin
lemon twist, to garnish

Add all ingredients (except the lemon twist) to a cocktail shaker with some ice cubes. Shake for 10–15 seconds and strain into a martini glass.

Serve garnished with the lemon twist.

NEGRONI

MAKES 1

Jock always had various ice shapes and sizes in the freezer to make sure he made the ultimate cocktail. His negroni was always over square ice. His orange rind would have absolutely no sign of white pith on the underside, and he would rub it around the rim, then push it down the side between the glass and the ice so it didn't hit your face.

1 shot (30 ml) gin (Jock liked The Botanist Islay Dry Gin or Drumshanbo Gunpowder Irish Gin)
1 shot (30 ml) sweet vermouth
1 shot (30 ml) Campari
1 thin strip blood orange rind, to garnish

Combine the gin, sweet vermouth and Campari in a mixing glass filled with ice and stir well until cold. Strain into a tumbler and add a large ice cube.

Rub the glass rim with the blood orange rind then add to the glass.

KING'S CUT WHISKY

Jock would mainly drink single-malt Scottish whisky, and he built quite the collection. A lot of them were from ghost distilleries that are no longer in production, but he also gravitated to Mortlach, The Balvenie, Glenmorangie and Glenfarclas. Never a peaty whisky – he wouldn't ever allow that to be in his glass.

As the bottles started to get low, there wouldn't be enough to pour one for himself and me (again, it was a heavy pour), so Jock would combine all of the bottles that were almost empty in a decanter and it would be his king's cut.

PACIFIC OYSTERS
WITH SICILIAN OLIVE MIGNONETTE

SERVES 4

1 eschalot, finely diced

4–5 Sicilian olives, pitted and finely diced

1 tbsp chives, finely sliced

⅓ cup (80 ml) apple cider vinegar

1¾ tbsp olive brine

1 tbsp jalapeño hot sauce (optional)

12 freshly shucked Pacific oysters

In a bowl, mix the eschalot, olives and chives with the apple cider vinegar, olive brine and jalapeño hot sauce, if using. Add freshly ground black pepper – the more, the better – and mix well.

Next, loosen the oysters from their shells and flip them over so they are all presentation-side up. Serve the oysters on a large platter of ice with the mignonette sauce in a bowl in the middle. Spoon a little sauce on each oyster and serve.

'Brine is magic, never throw it out.'

Credit: Lauren Zonfrillo

STUFFED FRIED SICILIAN OLIVES

SERVES 6

vegetable oil, for deep-frying

100 g sausages, casings removed

1 tbsp 'nduja (spicy, spreadable salami)

¼ cup (25 g) finely grated parmesan

juice of ½ lemon

230 g jar pitted Sicilian olives

flour, for coating

1 egg, whisked

breadcrumbs, for coating

Fill a medium-sized pot no more than halfway with oil and heat to 196°C.

Meanwhile, make the filling: in a small bowl, combine the sausage meat, 'nduja, parmesan and lemon juice and mix well. Spoon into a piping bag fitted with a small nozzle.

Empty your jar of olives, reserving the brine to use in another dish (it's great in dressings, sauces and marinades). Pipe in a small amount of filling to completely fill the olive. It's important that you pack this in tight – you don't want air bubbles.

Place the flour, egg and breadcrumbs in individual bowls. Roll the stuffed olives in the flour (remove excess flour by rolling them around gently in your fingers), then dunk them in the egg to fully coat, then roll them in the breadcrumbs.

Carefully place the olives in the hot oil. They will bubble rapidly in the oil the whole time, so keep an eye on them, moving them often until they're golden brown all over.

Remove and drain on paper towel, then serve. The olives will be super hot, so give them a little bit of time to rest and cool before popping a whole one in your mouth!

Jock travelling in Peru, in October 2018.

'The knowledge we find in these Indigenous communities, which they've been keeping for a long time, is going to be very important in the future.'

FOCACCIA
WITH SEMI-DRIED TOMATOES, OLIVES AND ROSEMARY OIL

MAKES 1 FOCACCIA

130 ml extra-virgin olive oil, plus extra, for greasing
2 large rosemary sprigs
500 g bread flour
2 tsp salt
7 g sachet instant yeast with bread improver
290 ml warm water
60 g semi-dried tomatoes
50 g black olives, pitted

Start by greasing a mixing bowl and your baking tray (roughly 30 x 26 x 3 cm) with olive oil. No dry corners – this dough loves oil.

In a small saucepan, heat the olive oil to 80°C. Strip the rosemary leaves, chop them roughly and add to the oil. Let it infuse while it cools down, then strain it to remove the herbs and it's ready to use.

In a large mixing bowl, combine the flour and salt. Make a well in the middle, pour in the yeast and warm water, and whisk gently to dissolve, pulling in a bit of flour as you go. Add 70 ml of the cooled rosemary oil and whisk again, folding in more flour. Then use your hands or a pastry scraper to bring it all together into a rough, sticky dough.

Turn it out onto a clean bench (or use a stand mixer if you like) and knead for 10 minutes until it's smooth and elastic.

Pop the dough into your oiled bowl, cover with a tea towel and let it rise in a warm spot for about 45 minutes or until doubled in size.

Once it's puffed, gently tip the dough into your oiled tray and stretch it out to the edges with your fingers. Press in the semi-dried tomatoes and olives, then drizzle with a bit more rosemary oil. Cover again and leave to rise for another 30–45 minutes, until pillowy.

Preheat your oven to 200°C. When it's ready to bake, drizzle the top generously with rosemary oil, sprinkle with flaked salt, and press your fingers in to create a few deep divots. Let it rest another 10 minutes, then bake for 20–25 minutes until golden and crisp on top.

Brush with any leftover rosemary oil and let it cool a bit on a wire rack. You can serve this warm by itself, fill it with some mortadella or prosciutto, or as a side for another meal.

Credit: Lauren Zonfrillo

'Focaccia is one of my favourite breads. Crunchy on the outside and pillowy soft on the inside, it's a recipe my family comes back to time and time again, either plain or with some beautiful olives and sundried tomatoes tucked in. I assure you, it's easy to master and will become your new go-to.'

BAGNA CAUDA
WITH CRUDITÉS AND CRUNCHY BREAD

SERVES 4

FOR THE BAGNA CAUDA

- scant ¾ cup (160 ml) extra-virgin olive oil
- 70 g anchovies in oil, roughly chopped
- 12 garlic cloves, finely sliced
- juice and pulp of 1 lemon, plus a little more lemon juice
- 5 tbsp (100 ml) water

FOR THE CRUDITÉS

- 2–3 radishes
- 2–3 baby zucchini
- ½ red witlof
- 1–2 baby fennel bulbs
- 1 bunch asparagus
- 1–2 celery stalks
- 1 red capsicum
- 1 packet rosemary and sea salt grissini
- 1 packet olive oil and sea salt crustini

In a small saucepan, add the olive oil, anchovies, garlic, and the juice and pulp of the lemon. Cook it low and slow – the key here is *not* to fry anything. Stir often, and let it gently bubble away for about 15 minutes, or until the garlic is soft and the anchovies have melted into the oil.

Once everything's silky and mellow, blitz it with a stick blender until smooth. Add the water and a little more lemon juice to loosen it up to your liking. Pour into a bowl and set aside.

For the crudités, slice the radishes, zucchini, witlof, fennel, asparagus, celery and capsicum into whatever shapes you like for dipping. Blanch the zucchini and asparagus if you want them a bit softer – totally your call.

Arrange everything on a big platter with some rosemary grissini and olive oil crustini. Pop the warm bagna cauda in the middle for dipping.

It's garlicky, anchovy-rich and salty in the best way.

'This is pretty much a garlic and anchovy dip for whatever you have kicking around the kitchen. Traditionally, the bagna cauda is kept warm as you dip away, but you can dunk into it cold, it's still delicious.'

MONDEGHILI MEATBALLS
WITH GREMOLATA

SERVES 6–8

vegetable oil, for deep frying

FOR THE MEATBALLS

1 slice white bread, crusts removed

¼ cup (60 ml) milk

200 g pork mince

50 g pork sausage, casings removed and meat torn into chunks

50 g mortadella, grated

1 egg

¼ bunch flat-leaf parsley, finely chopped

1 garlic clove, minced

¼ cup (25 g) finely grated parmesan

pinch of nutmeg

1 cup (100 g) panko breadcrumbs

FOR THE GREMOLATA

1 bunch parsley, roughly chopped

zest and juice of 1 lemon

zest and juice of ½ orange

1½ tbsp extra-virgin olive oil

3 tsp red wine vinegar

1 garlic clove, minced

Heat your oil to 160°C in a large pot – don't fill it more than halfway.

To make the gremolata, combine all the ingredients in a bowl: parsley, lemon zest and juice, orange zest and juice, olive oil, red wine vinegar and garlic. Give it a stir and set aside.

For the meatballs, start by soaking the bread in milk. Once it's soft, squeeze out the excess and dice it finely. In a bowl, mix it with the pork mince, sausage meat, mortadella, egg, parsley, garlic, parmesan and nutmeg. Season well with salt and pepper, and mix until everything's evenly combined.

Shape into eight puck-sized meatballs – about 50 g each – and coat each one in panko breadcrumbs. Press them in gently so the crumb sticks.

Fry the meatballs in batches until golden and cooked through, about 5 minutes per batch. Drain on paper towel.

Serve hot with a small bowl of gremolata on the side. Salty, crispy, lemony, yum.

TRIPLE-COOKED CHIPS

SERVES 4

4 extra-large potatoes

vegetable oil, for deep-frying

malt vinegar, to serve

Start by peeling your potatoes and cutting them into thick, finger-length chips – about 12 mm wide. Uniformity helps them cook evenly, so take your time here.

Fill a large, heavy-based pot with vegetable oil no more than halfway and heat it to 170°C.

Drop in your raw chips – the oil will drop in temp slightly, so bring it back up to around 163°C and fry until the chips just start to colour. You're not after golden yet, just a slight cook. Scoop them out and drain on a wire rack. That's round one.

Repeat this process two more times – each time, the chips get crispier and more golden. After the third fry, they should be deeply golden, crunchy on the outside and fluffy inside.

Season immediately with plenty of sea salt while they're still hot, and serve on a bit of newspaper with excessive amounts of malt vinegar drizzled over them.

'Also known as "Scottish salad".'

SNACKS AND COCKTAILS

TOMATO ARANCINI
WITH BASIL AND MOZZARELLA

MAKES 6

vegetable oil, for deep-frying

600 g leftover risotto, dry from being refrigerated

⅔ cup (120 g) triple-concentrate tomato paste

90 g mozzarella, cut into 5 cm batons

12 basil leaves

¾ cup (125 g) flour

2 eggs

5 tbsp (100 ml) milk

2 cups (200 g) panko breadcrumbs

Heat your oil to 180°C in a fryer or deep pot. Don't fill it more than halfway – hot oil needs space.

In a large bowl, mix your cold leftover risotto with the tomato paste. It should be stiff from the fridge – perfect for shaping.

Divide the mixture into six 100 g portions. Take one, flatten it in your palm, and press a baton of mozzarella and two basil leaves into the centre. Fold the rice around the filling and roll into a neat ball. Repeat with the rest.

Set up a crumbing station: flour in one tray, whisked eggs and milk in a bowl, and panko breadcrumbs in another. Roll each arancini ball in flour, then into the egg mix, then into the breadcrumbs. Press gently so the coating sticks.

Fry in batches for about 6 minutes or until golden and crisp all over. Drain on paper towel, hit them with salt, and let them cool just slightly before serving, these puppies are hot!

Credit: Lauren Zonfrillo

GNOCCHO FRITTO
WITH SHAVED MORTADELLA

SERVES 6–8

- ⅓ cup (80 ml) milk
- ⅓ cup (80 ml) water
- 1 tsp caster sugar
- ⅔ tsp instant dry yeast
- 2¼ cups (350 g) plain flour, sifted
- 1 tsp salt
- 50 g lard, at room temperature, diced
- vegetable oil, for deep-frying
- ¼ cup (25 g) finely grated Pecorino Romano, to serve
- 300 g shaved mortadella, to serve

In a small saucepan, heat the milk, water and sugar until just lukewarm, not hot. Whisk in the yeast and leave it for about 10 minutes until frothy.

In a big mixing bowl, combine the flour and salt. Make a well in the middle and pour in the yeast mixture along with the diced lard. Mix everything together until you've got a soft dough.

Tip it onto the bench and knead for about 5 minutes until smooth, elastic and springy. Shape into a ball, cover with a clean, damp tea towel and leave to rise in a warm place for 2 hours, or until doubled in size.

Once the dough's risen, roll it out on a floured surface to about 5 mm thick. Use a pasta wheel or knife to cut it into 2.5 cm squares.

Heat your oil to 180°C in a deep pot – no more than halfway full. Fry the dough squares in batches for 1½ to 2 minutes, until they puff up and turn golden. Turn them halfway to get an even colour.

Drain on paper towel, season with salt and pepper, and toss gently to coat. Serve warm, piled high with plenty of finely grated Pecorino and a stack of shaved mortadella on the side.

SNACKS AND COCKTAILS

SALT AND PEPPER BUGS

SERVES 4

500 g Moreton Bay or Balmain bug tail meat
4 cups (600 g) potato flour
1¼ cups (200 g) cornflour
⅔ cup (100 g) tapioca flour
1 tsp salt
1 egg white
1 lemon, plus extra, to season
vegetable oil, for deep-frying
1 red chilli, finely sliced

First, prep your bugs. Cut the tail meat into halves or quarters, depending on how big they are. Give them a quick rinse and pat dry with paper towel.

In a large bowl, mix together the potato flour, cornflour, tapioca flour and salt. In a separate bowl, whisk the egg white until frothy. Toss the bug meat in the egg white, then coat it in the flour mix, massaging it gently so every little crevice is coated. This is where the crisp comes from.

Squeeze the juice of half a lemon over the floured meat, flip, and hit the other side too – it gives the batter a clean citrus lift when it fries which is delicious.

Heat your oil to 190°C. Fry the bug pieces in small batches for about 4 minutes until just golden. Drain on paper towel.

Once they're all cooked, crank the oil back up to 190°C and give them a second fry – just 60 to 90 seconds – until they're deep golden and shatteringly crisp, and drain on paper towel again.

Season with more salt, pepper and a final squeeze of lemon. Scatter over the sliced red chilli and serve them up while they're still hot and crackly.

'A great alternative to fish and chips.'

Quick AND BASIC

SPECK AND PRAWN KIMCHI FRIED RICE

SERVES 4

6 tiger prawns, peeled and deveined
5 tbsp (100 ml) kimchi juice plus 1 cup (180 g) kimchi, roughly chopped
2 eggs
1 tbsp gochujang (Korean chilli paste)
1½ tbsp light soy sauce
2 tsp rice wine vinegar
1 tsp fish sauce
2 tsp sesame oil
2½ tsp sugar
3 cups (500 g) cooked white rice
200 g speck or streaky bacon, cut into lardons
4 spring onions, thinly sliced, white and green parts separated
2 nori sheets, cut into thin strips
toasted sesame seeds, to serve

Start by slicing the prawns into 3 cm chunks and marinating them in the kimchi juice. Let them sit while you get everything else going.

In a large bowl, whisk together the eggs, gochujang, soy sauce, rice vinegar, fish sauce, sesame oil, sugar and a pinch of white pepper. Pour this mixture over the cold rice and get in there with your hands to break up any clumps and make sure every grain gets coated.

Place a frying pan over medium–high heat and add the speck to the cold pan – this lets the fat slowly render as the pan heats. Cook until golden, then scoop it out with a slotted spoon and put into a bowl with paper towel to drain, leaving the rendered fat in the pan.

Turn the heat up to high and add the chopped kimchi. Stir-fry briefly, then strain the prawns from the kimchi juice and toss them into the pan with the white parts of the spring onion. Fry until the prawns just start to colour.

Add in the rice mixture and stir-fry until it's hot and starting to catch in places – you want those crispy bits. Fold in the nori strips and cook until just wilted.

Serve hot, topped with the green parts of the spring onion and a sprinkle of toasted sesame seeds.

COTTAGE CHEESE AND SPINACH POCKETS
WITH SPICED HONEY

MAKES 2

FOR THE DOUGH

1 heaped cup (180 g) bread flour, plus more for dusting

pinch of salt

20 g butter, chopped

scant ½ cup (110 ml) milk

FOR THE COTTAGE CHEESE FILLING

scant ½ cup (125 g) cottage cheese

1 cup (125 g) mashed potato

50 g baby spinach, sauteed

zest of 1 lemon

1 tbsp finely chopped thyme

FOR THE SPICED HONEY

2 tbsp honey

1 birdseye chilli, finely sliced

juice of ½ lemon

butter, for frying

To make the dough, mix the flour and a pinch of salt in a large bowl. Rub in the butter with your fingertips until it resembles crumbs. Make a well in the centre, pour in the milk, and stir through until a dough forms. Turn it out onto a floured bench and knead for 5 minutes until smooth and elastic. Pop it into a clean bowl, cover with cling film and rest at room temperature for 1 hour.

While that's resting, make the filling by folding together the cottage cheese, mashed potato, sauteed spinach, lemon zest and thyme. Keep it gentle, you don't want it too loose, then divide it into two equal portions.

For the spiced honey, bring the honey and sliced chilli to a simmer in a small saucepan. Remove from the heat, stir through the lemon juice and set it aside to cool.

Once the dough has rested, divide it in two and roll each piece into a 25 cm circle. Place the filling in the centre of each, forming a tight 10 cm mound. Fold the dough up and over the filling, pinch to seal, then flip the whole thing so the seam is underneath. Gently flatten into a disc using a rolling pin.

Heat a generous amount of butter in a frying pan over medium heat. Fry one pocket at a time until golden and crisp on both sides – about 3 minutes each side. Let them rest for a moment, then slice into quarters and serve with that spiced honey on the side.

'This is super easy to whip up with ingredients you've probably got in the kitchen. Its golden, crispy outside and rich, cheesy filling never fails. Plus, once you learn how to make the dough, you can mix anything with cottage cheese for a different filling. So get stuck into it!'

CRISPY SHREDDED BEEF

SERVES 4

500 g beef sirloin or rump

1 tsp baking soda

1 brown onion, roughly chopped

2 garlic cloves, sliced

10 g ginger, sliced

1 tbsp light soy sauce

1¼ cups (200 g) potato flour

½ cup (100 g) cornflour

vegetable oil, for deep frying

2 spring onions, finely sliced, to serve

1 tsp toasted sesame seeds, to serve

FOR THE SAUCE

¾ cup (250 g) honey

2 tbsp hoisin sauce

½ cup water

½ tbsp dark soy sauce

4 tbsp light soy sauce

1½ tbsp Shaoxing wine

30 g crispy chilli oil (see page 12)

2 tbsp red wine vinegar

3 tsp Sichuan peppercorns, toasted and ground

1 tbsp cornflour

Start by slicing the beef into thin strips – about 10 cm long and 5 mm wide. Toss with the baking soda and leave it to tenderise while you sort the rest.

In a blender or with a stick blender, blitz the onion, garlic, ginger and light soy sauce until smooth. Pour that over the beef, mix well, and let it marinate for an hour.

Once it's had time to soak, mix the potato and cornflour in a bowl and coat the beef pieces thoroughly. Let them sit in the flour mix for 15–20 minutes while you get the sauce going.

In a saucepan or wok, combine the honey, hoisin, 100 ml water, dark soy, light soy, Shaoxing wine, chilli oil, red wine vinegar and toasted Sichuan pepper. Bring to a simmer and reduce for 5–6 minutes until slightly thickened. Mix the cornflour with a tablespoon of water to make a slurry, then whisk it into the sauce. Simmer until glossy, then take it off the heat.

Heat the oil to 170°C in a heavy-based pot – no more than halfway full. Fry the beef in a single batch at around 160°C for 5–6 minutes until golden brown. Remove, drain on paper towel, and rest for 5 minutes.

Crank the oil back up to 190°C and fry the beef again for another minute to really crisp it up. Drain again and toss it through the warm sauce until coated.

Serve hot, sprinkled with spring onion and sesame seeds.

Jock with English Longhorn cattle in the Adelaide Hills, South Australia, in June 2015.
Credit: Jacqui Way

'There isn't a great deal of room for creativity when you're at the bottom of the ladder in the food world.

For example, at Turnberry, they wouldn't let me anywhere near the meat section or teach me how to cook meat properly until they judged me skilled enough, because it was too expensive to risk fucking up. I found this really frustrating because I wanted to know everything there was to know about food, right then, right there.'

CHILLI OIL CRAB NOODLES

SERVES 2–3

250 g fresh thick wheat noodles (or egg or rice noodles)

2 tbsp crispy chilli oil (see page 12), plus extra, to serve

2 handfuls coriander, chopped, plus extra, to serve

1 handful mint, chopped, plus extra, to serve

1 cup shredded cooked white crab meat

½ cup shredded cooked brown crab meat (or use extra white crab meat)

Bring a pot of water to the boil and cook the noodles according to the packet instructions. Drain and set aside.

In a frying pan over medium heat, warm the chilli oil until it just starts to bubble. Add the noodles to the pan along with the chopped coriander and mint. Toss everything together so the noodles are coated and glistening.

Take it off the heat and fold through the crab meat – both white and brown if you're using both. Be gentle here, you want to keep the crab intact.

Serve straight into bowls, then drizzle over a bit more chilli oil and scatter with the rest of the mint and coriander. It's spicy, silky and packed with flavour.

PIPERADE

SERVES 2

- 1 capsicum, deseeded and sliced
- 2 tsp extra-virgin olive oil
- 150 g guanciale, diced
- 1 large onion, sliced
- 3–4 garlic cloves, sliced
- 2 tsp Aleppo pepper (see Note)
- 1½ tsp Espelette pepper (see Note)
- 1½ tsp sweet paprika
- 1½ tsp smoked paprika
- 4 eggs
- 1 baguette

Start by slicing the capsicum, salting it, and letting it sit for 20 minutes. This draws out moisture so it cooks down without going soggy.

Heat the olive oil in a pan over medium heat and add the guanciale. Let it render a bit, then throw in the onion, garlic, Aleppo and Espelette pepper, sweet and smoked paprika. Cook gently until the onion and garlic are soft and caramelised – no rushing here.

Once the capsicum's had its time, squeeze out the excess moisture and add it to the pan. Stir it through, season well, and cook for another 5–6 minutes. You want it softened, not collapsed.

Crack your eggs into a bowl and whisk. Take the pan off the heat, pour in half the eggs and fold gently. Add the rest and return to a low heat, stirring constantly until the mixture becomes thick, glossy and velvety.

Serve straight away with slices of fresh baguette – no garnish, no faff. Just spoon and bread.

NOTE: *Aleppo pepper and Espelette pepper are types of dried chilli with a mild heat and fruity flavour. If you can't find them, add a little cayenne pepper or your preferred chilli flakes.*

'This is posh scrambled eggs that have a velvety, thick texture. As soon as you take it off the heat, serve it up with a fresh baguette – boom!'

QUICK AND BASIC

RISOTTO VERDE
WITH AGRODOLCE

SERVES 2

1 cup (200 g) carnaroli rice

1½ tbsp extra-virgin olive oil, plus extra, for drizzling

½ brown onion, finely diced

1 celery stick, finely diced

¼ cup (60 ml) white wine (ideally a dry, nutty and floral wine like fiano)

1 litre boiling water, plus extra, to loosen

¼ cup (50 g) crème fraîche

½ cup (40 g) finely grated Parmigiano Reggiano

squeeze of lemon juice

80 g broad beans, shelled and blanched, cooled to room temperature

80 g frozen peas, at room temperature

80 g green beans, blanched and sliced 1 cm thick

SALSA VERDE (SEE PAGE 20)

FOR THE AGRODOLCE

1¼ tbsp honey

juice of 1 lemon

Heat a heavy-based saucepan over medium heat and toast the rice dry – stir often until the grains go chalky and hot to the touch. Tip it out and set aside.

Lower the heat, add the olive oil and cook the diced onion and celery until soft and translucent – no colour, just sweet. Stir the rice back in and let it soak up the flavour.

Pour in the white wine and simmer until it's nearly all gone. Then start adding boiling water a ladle at a time, stirring constantly and letting each addition absorb before adding the next. After the first ladle, season with salt and white pepper.

Keep going until the rice is about three-quarters cooked. Take it off the heat, stir through the crème fraîche, Parmigiano and a squeeze of lemon juice. Cover with a clean tea towel and let it rest for 5 minutes – this is where it turns creamy.

While it's resting, warm the honey gently in a small pan, then stir in the lemon juice. That's your agrodolce done – sweet and sharp.

Put the pan back on low, fold in the green veggies and the salsa verde, and adjust the texture with more hot water – you want that beautiful, wave-like consistency. Finish with the agrodolce stirred through to balance the whole thing.

Serve immediately on warm plates, and don't hang about – risotto waits for no one.

CLASSIC SAUSAGE ROLLS

MAKES 16

1 slice old bread, crusts removed

a splash of milk

1½ tbsp grapeseed oil

1 large brown onion, finely diced

1 carrot, grated

2 garlic cloves, minced

1¼ tbsp ground fennel

2 rosemary sprigs, finely chopped

625 g Italian pork sausage, casings removed

1 egg

3 oregano sprigs, finely chopped

1 tbsp dijon mustard

1¼ tsp sweet paprika

1 egg yolk

1 tsp milk

2 sheets puff pastry

sesame seeds and fennel seeds, for sprinkling

Preheat your oven to 180°C and line a baking tray with baking paper.

Soak the bread in a splash of milk and set it aside to soften.

Heat the grapeseed oil in a frying pan over medium heat. Add the onion, carrot and garlic, and cook until soft and sweet. Stir in the fennel seeds and rosemary, and keep cooking until it all smells incredible and just starts to caramelise. Set aside to cool.

Squeeze the excess milk from the bread and tear it into small bits. In a big bowl, combine it with the sausage meat, cooled veg, egg, oregano, mustard and sweet paprika. Season generously and mix it all together well. Load it into a piping bag and snip a 6 cm hole at the tip.

Lay the puff pastry sheets on your bench and cut each in half. Pipe the filling in a neat line about a centimetre in from one edge. Brush the edge with egg wash, roll the pastry over the filling, and press to seal. Use a fork to crimp the seam closed.

Brush the tops with more egg wash and sprinkle with sesame and fennel seeds. Cut each roll into four to make sixteen pieces.

Place on the baking tray and bake for 20–25 minutes, turning once halfway through, until puffed and golden brown. They're everything a sausage roll should be – flaky, juicy, and yum.

'These bad boys trump the servo sausage roll with the addition of proper Italian pork sausage, but they still have a healthy amount of garlic and flecks of carrot to give it the signature look.

What sauce do you have with yours? I'm a HP man myself.'

VEGAN CHICKPEA GNOCCHI SARDI

SERVES 2

- 260 g gnocchi sardi or other short pasta
- extra-virgin olive oil, for frying
- 1 garlic clove, skin on
- 400 g canned chickpeas, drained, liquid reserved
- zest and juice of 1 lemon
- a few parsley sprigs, leaves picked
- a handful of sage leaves

Bring a pot of salted water to the boil and cook the pasta for 2 minutes less than the packet says – it will finish in the pan.

While that's going, heat a generous glug of olive oil in a frying pan over low heat. Smash the garlic clove (skin on) and toss it in with a good pinch of salt and pepper. Add the chickpeas and let them warm through. Stir in the lemon zest and cook for 3–4 minutes so everything mingles.

Add about 70 ml of the reserved chickpea liquid and a squeeze of lemon juice. If it still looks dry, add a bit more juice.

Drain the pasta over a mug and reserve some of the pasta water. Add the cooked pasta straight into the pan and stir to coat. Loosen with a splash of pasta water if needed.

Throw in the parsley and sage, and let them just wilt in the heat of the pan. Remove the garlic clove before serving, adjust the seasoning, and plate it up.

'This is one of my favourite pasta dishes and it's VEGAN!'

Jock cooking at Casa Olivetta in Puglia, Italy, in September 2022.
Credit: Lauren Zonfrillo

'Food has been my anchor. It's always been there, my entire life; the one constant. Whether it was looking forward to eating clootie dumpling at Nana's house or lasagne at Uncle Tony's, meals were the highlight of my day, and a very grounding thing.'

ITALIAN CANNELLINI BEAN AND CHICKEN SALAD

SERVES 2

- 2 x 400 g cans cannellini beans
- 1 garlic clove, minced
- 1 eschalot, finely diced
- 2 tbsp extra-virgin olive oil
- ¼ cup (60 ml) water
- pinch of salt
- ¼ tsp smoked paprika
- zest and juice of 1 lemon
- ⅓ cup black olives, chopped
- handful of basil leaves
- shio koji (natural flavour enhancer), to drizzle
- red wine vinegar, to drizzle
- 1 cup semi-dried tomatoes
- 500 g taleggio, cubed
- 1 poached chicken breast, sliced

Drain the cannellini beans over a bowl and keep the liquid – you'll use that in a minute.

In a frying pan over medium heat, cook the garlic and eschalot in olive oil and water until softened. Add a pinch of salt and the smoked paprika, stir well and let it cook for 2–3 minutes.

Pour in the reserved bean liquid and simmer until it reduces by half. Stir through the lemon zest and juice, half the olives, the basil, and the beans. Mix gently so the beans stay whole.

Take it off the heat and drizzle with a little shio koji and red wine vinegar. Add the semi-dried tomatoes and cubed taleggio, and stir gently just to combine.

Lay the sliced poached chicken breast over the top and finish with the remaining olives and a few torn basil leaves. Best served warm or at room temp.

'I made this on the fly one day and never wrote the ingredients down, but I think this is it ...'

STEAK SANDWICH
WITH SMOKY PEPPER BEER GLAZE

SERVES 4

4 x 160 g–200 g wagyu skirt steaks
2 tbsp grapeseed oil, plus extra, for grilling
3 brown onions, finely sliced
1 garlic clove, finely sliced
2 fresh bay leaves
330 ml bottle pale ale
4 Turkish bread rolls or soft ciabatta rolls
butter, for spreading
2 baby cos lettuce, finely shredded
1 ripe tomato, thinly sliced

FOR THE SMOKY PEPPER BEER GLAZE

1 tbsp grapeseed oil
1 small brown onion, diced
2 garlic cloves, peeled and crushed
2 tsp freshly cracked black pepper
1¼ tbsp raw sugar
2 tsp oyster sauce
5 tbsp (100 ml) dark soy sauce
5 tbsp (100 ml) smoky barbecue sauce
20 g candlenuts, crushed
1 bottle golden ale

Firstly and most importantly, take the steaks out of the fridge at least 20 minutes before cooking to bring to room temperature. Season with salt and pepper.

Next, make the smoky pepper beer glaze. Heat grapeseed oil in a medium-sized saucepan over medium heat. Add onion and stir until it starts to soften. Add garlic and cook until translucent, then add pepper, sugar, oyster sauce, soy sauce, barbecue sauce and candlenuts and cook until the mixture starts to catch in the bottom of the pan. Deglaze with the golden ale, making sure to scrape the bottom of the pan well. Continue to cook until it reduces to a thick paste. Remove from heat and blitz with a stick blender until smooth. Set aside.

Heat some grapeseed oil in a large frying pan over medium heat. Add the sliced onion and stir constantly for the first minute or so. As the onion starts to soften, add the garlic and bay leaves. Keep stirring until the onion is golden brown and starts sticking to the base of the pan. Pour in the pale ale and simmer on low heat to reduce until the pan is almost dry and the onion is caramelised. Remove the bay leaves and discard.

Heat a hibachi, barbecue or grill pan to smoking hot. Rub the steaks with a little grapeseed oil, then cook for a minute or so on each side until they start to caramelise all over. Reduce the heat and cook until the internal temperature is 48°C. At the same time, slice the bread rolls in half and place cut-side down on the grill until toasted. Remove the steaks from the heat and rest for at least 5 minutes.

To assemble the sandwich, place a toasted bread roll open on a cutting board, butter the toasted sides lightly and spread caramelised onion on both pieces. Next, add shredded lettuce on the bottom followed by a single layer of tomato and season lightly with salt and pepper. Slice a steak at a 45-degree angle and place on top of the tomato, drizzle liberally with the smoky pepper beer glaze, and gently place the bread roll lid on top. Repeat with the remaining ingredients to make four sandwiches.

PEA, CUCUMBER AND CELERY SALAD

SERVES 4, AS A SIDE

1 cup fresh peas, blanched and cooled

1 cup fresh edamame beans, blanched and cooled

200 g sugar snap peas, trimmed and sliced on a diagonal

200 g snow peas, trimmed and sliced on a diagonal

1 cucumber, halved, seeds removed and sliced on a diagonal

1 celery stick, peeled to remove strings, sliced on a diagonal

FOR THE DRESSING

2 tbsp grapeseed oil

2 tbsp apple cider vinegar or lemon juice

Combine all salad ingredients in a large bowl.

Place dressing ingredients in a small bowl or jar, season with salt and pepper and whisk or shake to combine. Pour over the salad, toss gently and serve.

SAUTÉED SPINACH WITH DIJON

SERVES 2–3, AS A SIDE

20 g butter

1 large bag baby spinach (around 7–8 handfuls)

1 tsp dijon mustard

Heat a frying pan over medium heat and melt the butter. Add the spinach and a dash of water and sauté until nearly wilted. Add the mustard and stir through over the heat and serve.

CLASSIC VINAIGRETTE SALAD

SERVES 2–3, AS A SIDE

1 butter lettuce, washed and leaves separated

FOR THE VINAIGRETTE

1½ tbsp grapeseed oil

1½ tbsp apple cider vinegar

1½ tsp white soy sauce

pinch of white pepper

pinch of caster sugar

To make the vinaigrette dressing, whisk all ingredients together in a small bowl or shake in a jar.

Place the lettuce in a bowl or on a platter and pour over the dressing. Toss gently and serve.

BABY GEM WITH SPICY GUACAMOLE

SERVES 2, AS A SIDE

1–2 baby gem lettuces, washed and leaves separated

FOR THE SPICY GUACAMOLE

1 avocado, diced into 5 mm cubes

¼ bunch chives, finely sliced

zest and juice of 1 lime

1–2 tsp fermented hot sauce (like Tabasco or sriracha), to taste

To make the spicy guacamole, combine all ingredients in a bowl, season with salt and white pepper to taste and mix gently.

Then serve by spooning the guacamole onto the lettuce cups and eat.

Posh SALADS

BISTRO SALAD
WITH JOCK'S FRENCH DRESSING

SERVES 4

1 butter lettuce, washed and leaves separated

1 eschalot, thinly sliced and soaked in lemon juice

1 bunch radish, thinly sliced

FOR THE DRESSING

1 egg yolk

1 tsp dijon mustard

2½ tbsp grapeseed oil

1 tbsp rice wine vinegar

2 tsp white soy sauce

pinch of white pepper

To make the dressing, whisk the egg yolk and dijon mustard in a bowl until light and airy. Slowly stream in the grapeseed oil while whisking to form an emulsion. Once that's silky, whisk in the rice wine vinegar, white soy sauce and a pinch of white pepper. Taste and tweak if needed.

Arrange the butter lettuce leaves on a platter. Scatter over the lemon-soaked eschalot slices and the radish. Drizzle the dressing generously over the top, letting it fall into all the nooks of the lettuce.

CAESAR SALAD
WITH LEFTOVER ROAST CHICKEN
SERVES 2

120 g speck, thinly sliced

2 baby cos lettuces, washed and separated into leaves

2 cups leftover roast chicken, shredded

2 soft-boiled eggs, quartered

6 anchovies, split lengthways

½ cup (50 g) finely grated parmesan

FOR THE CAESAR DRESSING

½ garlic clove

2–3 cornichons

2 tsp capers

1½ tbsp dijon mustard

2 tbsp anchovies

2 egg yolks

1½ tbsp lemon juice, plus extra, to taste

1 tbsp apple cider vinegar

1 tsp Worcestershire sauce

a few dashes of Tabasco

200 ml grapeseed oil

FOR THE CROUTONS

90 g stale bread, crusts removed

1 tbsp extra-virgin olive oil

5 tbsp (100 ml) apple cider vinegar

Preheat the oven to 160°C.

To make the caesar dressing, use a stick blender or food processor to puree all the ingredients, except the oil, until smooth. Gradually pour in the oil while blending to emulsify. Season with salt, white pepper and, if needed, extra lemon juice to taste.

For the croutons, tear bread into irregular chunks. Toss in a bowl with the olive oil, vinegar, salt and pepper, then bake for about 10 minutes until deeply golden. Remove from the oven and let cool.

Increase the oven to 200°C. Arrange the speck slices in a single layer, sandwiched between two baking trays. Bake for 15–20 minutes or until crispy.

To make the salad, coat the lettuce leaves and shredded chicken with a few spoonfuls of caesar dressing and arrange on a plate. Drizzle some extra dressing on top – it's your call how much you add.

Arrange the boiled eggs on top, then the croutons, crispy speck and anchovies. Finish with freshly grated parmesan.

NOTE: *This recipe makes more dressing than you'll need, but trust me – you'll use it!*

'There are so many great ways to use up leftover roast chicken but I reckon caesar salad is the best. It's a thrifty way to make the most of the odd bits left on a whole roast chicken and get something on the table fast. Add in some baby cos lettuce, croutons, speck, parmesan and anchovies, and you've got a salad fit for a king.'

Jock at sunset on Nyul Nyul Country in the Dampier Peninsula, the Kimberley, Western Australia, in April 2019.
Credit: Lauren Zonfrillo

'Out there, in the middle of nowhere, with just a fire, the stars and good company, I feel completely at peace. It strips life back to what truly matters.'

HARISSA TUNA
WITH ROASTED VEGETABLE SALAD
SERVES 2

FOR THE HARISSA (MAKES 900 G)

1 head garlic
2 tsp grapeseed oil, plus extra, for drizzling
60 g dried ancho chillies
60 g dried guajillo chillies
peel and juice of 4 blood oranges
peel and juice of 2 lemons
peel and juice of 1 ruby grapefruit
3 tbsp (60 g) tomato paste
40 g preserved lemon, finely chopped
3 tbsp (50 g) raw sugar
2 tsp smoked paprika
3 tsp cumin seeds
1 tbsp caraway seeds
1½ tbsp coriander seeds
¼ cup (60 ml) red wine vinegar

Preheat the oven to 180°C.

For the harissa, cut the top off of the head of a bunch of garlic and place on top of a piece of foil. Drizzle with a splash of grapeseed oil and a pinch of salt then wrap tightly in the foil. Bake until soft, which will take about 30–45 minutes. The delicious smell will keep you company.

Spread out the dried chillies and citrus peels on a baking tray and roast until the chillies are beginning to darken. Place in a pot of boiling water and simmer for 15–20 minutes or until softened.

In a medium saucepan, heat 2 teaspoons grapeseed oil over medium heat. Add the tomato paste, citrus juices, preserved lemon, sugar and paprika and bring to a simmer.

Meanwhile, toast the spices in a dry pan over high heat until aromatic. Finely crush in a mortar and pestle, then add to the tomato paste mixture. Squeeze the roasted garlic into the saucepan. Simmer until the harissa is thick and dark burgundy in colour.

Strain the dried chillies and citrus peel, discarding the chilli stems. Finely chop the chillies and peel and add to the harissa. Add the red wine vinegar and then season with salt and pepper. Cover and continue to simmer for another 10 minutes.

Crank your oven up to 300°C (or as hot as it goes) and place a cast-iron grill pan inside to preheat. I do this in my woodfired pizza oven, so if you have one then I suggest you use that, but an oven is just as effective but sadly not as fun.

ROASTED VEGETABLE SALAD

80 g green beans, trimmed
40 g runner beans, trimmed
1 cayenne chilli
3 red banana chillies
2 green banana chillies
3 red baby capsicum
3 yellow baby capsicum
3 red bullhorn peppers
grapeseed oil, for coating
80 g broad beans, blanched and podded
60 g pitted green olives, halved
60 g treviso radicchio leaves, halved
60 g baby spinach
1 tbsp red wine vinegar
1½ tbsp extra-virgin olive oil
2 x 200 g tuna loin steaks

To make the salad, coat the green beans, runner beans, chillies and capsicums with oil, salt and pepper, and place on the hot grill pan. Roast until charred and just tender (you may need to do this in batches). Place the grill pan back in the oven to keep hot. This is a lot of touching the hot grill pan so go slow and steady.

Halve and deseed the banana chillies and capsicums and chop into bite-sized pieces. Destem and deseed the cayenne chilli and cut into 5 mm slices. Then combine with the beans, broad beans, olives, treviso and spinach. Dress with red wine vinegar, extra-virgin olive oil and salt to taste – there's lots of stages for seasoning, and the harisssa that goes on the tuna is also seasoned, so go light. Layer in a serving dish, bit by bit, spooning over dollops of harissa as you go.

Now onto the simplest bit – brush the tuna steaks on all sides with extra-virgin olive oil and season with salt flakes. Place on the hot grill pan and sear in the oven for up to 10 minutes. You want it just to sear and still be raw but warm through. Flip and brush the surface with harissa – get as much on there as you can – then place on top of the roasted vegetable salad and serve.

'Beautiful fresh tuna, an array of market vegetables, and some heat from my harissa sauce. This is the kind of salad I can get into!'

Credit: Lauren Zonfrillo

SQUID SALAD
WITH CASSAVA CRACKERS
SERVES 2

vegetable oil, for deep-frying
6 cassava crackers
1 lebanese cucumber
1 tsp rice wine vinegar
½ bunch coriander
400 g squid with tentacles, cleaned
grapeseed oil, for frying
1 tbsp Chinese barbecue sauce
1 tbsp nasi lemak sambal
juice of 1 lime
½ bunch mint, leaves torn

Fill a heavy-based pot no more than halfway with vegetable oil and heat to 180°C.

When the oil is hot, fry the cassava crackers at 180°C until puffed and crispy. Set aside, maybe eat a little bit to get you through.

Halve the cucumber, scrape a spoon down it lengthways to remove the seeds, then cut again so you have quartered it. Toss with a pinch of salt and a splash of rice wine vinegar. Set aside.

Cut the stems from the coriander and finely chop. Pick the leaves with a little stem and set aside.

Cut the squid on an angle into 1–2 cm slices and pat dry with paper towel.

Now we cook – heat a splash of grapeseed oil in a frying pan over high heat until smoking hot. Fry the squid for 15 seconds then add the barbecue sauce and nasi lemak sambal and fry briefly until aromatic. Add lime juice and coriander stems, stir through, then remove from the heat and transfer to a mixing bowl.

Drain the cucumber and add to the mixing bowl along with the coriander leaves and mint. Crush the cassava crackers into bite-sized pieces and sprinkle over the top. Give the salad a quick toss and serve so your squid is still warm.

'Good weather means salads, outside, barbecues ... Here's a zingy squid salad packed full of flavour, with only a few ingredients.'

TOMATO SALAD
WITH GRILLED PEACH, RICOTTA AND LEMON GRANITA

SERVES 4, AS A SIDE

6 flat peaches
extra-virgin olive oil, for drizzling
300 g tomatoes, roughly chopped
2 tbsp apple cider vinegar
250 g fresh ricotta
juice of 1 lemon, plus a little extra

FOR THE GRANITA

½ cup (100 g) raw caster sugar
1¼ cups (300 ml) water
200 ml lemon juice
pinch of salt

FOR THE BASIL OIL

150 g basil leaves
50 g spinach
1 cup (250 ml) grapeseed oil

To make the granita, in a small pan over high heat, bring the sugar and water to a boil then remove from the heat and add lemon juice and a pinch of salt. Transfer to a small tray and lay flat in your freezer. This is a useful recipe to know because it's also a super fast and refreshing dessert on its own or over a fruit salad.

Preheat the oven to as high as it will go – at least 250°C – so it's heating while you make the basil oil and prep the fruit and veggies.

To make the basil oil, place all ingredients in a blender and blitz for 2–3 minutes until the oil is bright green. Pass through a muslin cloth, Superbag or coffee filter into a bowl that's sitting in an ice bath. Stir so that it cools as quickly as possible.

Cut the peaches in half, remove the seed, and drizzle with extra-virgin olive oil and season with salt and white pepper. Place cut-side down on a cast-iron grill pan (if you are using this, preheat in the oven) or a baking tray and roast until blistered. Set aside to cool a little.

Place your tomatoes in a bowl and add the apple cider vinegar, salt and black pepper. Leave to macerate for 10 minutes. Meanwhile, cut the ricotta into wedges, place upright on a plate, and drizzle with lemon juice, extra-virgin olive oil, salt and black pepper.

Combine the tomatoes and cooled peaches and adjust seasoning to taste with extra lemon juice, salt and pepper. Transfer to a serving dish, then place ricotta across the salad, and finish with a good drizzle of basil oil. Run a fork through the lemon granita to create crystals, sprinkle over the salad and tell everyone to get to the table straight away!

'Warm, blistered flat peaches, fresh ricotta, icy lemon granita and basil oil makes for a wickedly good salad that's actually rather refreshing. You'll be counting down the days till you can make it again.'

BROCCOLI, JALAPEÑO AND SMOKED ALMOND SALAD

SERVES 4

2 large broccoli heads

⅓ cup (50 g) sunflower seeds

⅓ cup (50 g) pumpkin seeds

⅓ cup (50 g) smoked almonds

1 tsp smoked salt

2–3 sprigs mint, leaves picked

FOR THE DRESSING

1½ tbsp extra-virgin olive oil

1 tbsp white soy sauce

juice and zest of 1 lemon

2 tsp jalapeño hot sauce, plus extra, to taste

Cut the broccoli into 5 cm florets, then peel the broccoli stem and slice thinly on a diagonal.

Bring a pot of salted water to boil and blanch the florets for 1–2 minutes, be gentle with them so they don't fall apart. Refresh in a bowl of iced water. Drain and pat dry, or gently use a salad spinner.

Toast the sunflower and pumpkin seeds in a dry pan over medium heat until golden, don't walk away as these need constant attention. Then put the smoked almonds in a bowl or a mortar and pestle and lightly crush them, you still want them being chunky.

Whisk together all the ingredients for the dressing or put in a jar and shake. This is where you need to taste it and decide on your spice level – add more hot sauce if you like.

Combine the broccoli florets and stem, seeds, almonds and smoked salt in a large bowl. Tear the mint leaves over the top and drizzle with the dressing, toss gently then serve.

Jock during service at Orana in Residence,
Sydney, Australia, in September 2019.
Credit: Nikki To

'Restaurant Orana really has been the little restaurant that could. Other than my children, Orana opening, surviving and thriving is without question what I am most proud of in my life.

'It is my life's purpose to stand hand in hand with our Indigenous brothers and sisters, acknowledging that their culture is important and the beating heart of Australia.'

PANZANELLA SALAD
WITH THE ULTIMATE CROUTONS

SERVES 2

- 90 g stale bread, crusts removed
- ½ cup (125 ml) extra-virgin olive oil
- 4½ tbsp (90 ml) red wine vinegar
- ½ red onion, finely sliced
- juice of 2 lemons
- 1 garlic clove, minced
- 10 anchovies, minced
- 300 g cherry Roma tomatoes, halved
- 1 lebanese cucumber, cut into 1 cm chunks
- 3 tbsp (60 g) pitted marinated black olives
- ½ bunch basil, leaves picked

Preheat the oven to 160°C.

Tear the bread into chunks and toss in a bowl with 1 tbsp olive oil, 2½ tbsp red wine vinegar, salt and white pepper. Then spread them out on a baking tray and bake until deeply golden. This will take up to 15 minutes.

Meanwhile, soak the onion in the juice of 1 lemon until softened. 15 minutes minimum, if it's longer that is even better.

To make the dressing, heat 1 tablespoon of olive oil in a small saucepan over medium heat. Add the garlic and anchovies and start cooking down.

Squeeze the juice from the tomato halves through a fine strainer into the saucepan. Set the squeezed tomatoes aside. Simmer the dressing until thickened then remove from the heat and whisk in the remaining olive oil. Season with salt and pepper, add the juice of 1 lemon, then set aside.

In the bowl with the tomatoes, add the cucumber, salt, pepper and the remaining red wine vinegar. Leave to macerate for 10 minutes.

Give the cucumber, tomato and red onion a squeeze to remove extra liquid, then combine with the olives, basil leaves, croutons and dressing in a serving bowl. Toss gently and serve immediately.

'This will take you back to Italy, the lemons, olives, basil and anchovies making this a meal, not a side.'

NIÇOISE SALAD

SERVES 2

- 1 red onion, thinly sliced
- ½ cup (125 ml) red wine vinegar
- 2 lebanese cucumbers, peeled and halved lengthways
- 100 g cherry tomatoes
- 2 tsp extra-virgin olive oil
- 3 radishes, thinly sliced
- 100 g green beans, blanched and cut into thirds
- 2½ tbsp pitted marinated black olives, roughly chopped
- 1 tbsp olive brine
- ½ bunch basil, roughly chopped
- ½ head butter lettuce, washed and trimmed
- 140 g can good-quality tuna
- 2 soft-boiled eggs, quartered

FOR THE DRESSING

- 1 garlic clove
- 2½ tbsp extra-virgin olive oil
- 1½ tbsp red wine vinegar
- 1 tsp white soy sauce

I don't enjoy raw onion so to remove that taste, cover the sliced onion in 100 ml of red wine vinegar and leave to pickle for 15 minutes.

Cut the cucumber and cherry tomatoes into random bite-sized pieces, then dress with the remaining red wine vinegar, extra-virgin olive oil, salt and pepper. Set aside for 15 minutes to draw out the moisture.

To make the dressing, rub the garlic clove over the surface of a wooden mixing bowl, then discard. Combine the olive oil, vinegar, white soy sauce and freshly ground black pepper in the bowl and whisk, then pour into another bowl.

In the now-empty mixing bowl, toss together the radish, beans, olives and brine, basil, lettuce and tuna. Squeeze all the liquid from the pickled onion and add to the bowl, then strain the marinated cucumber and tomato and add to the bowl – reserve the liquid for the dressing.

Mix the reserved tomato and cucumber juice with the salad dressing and adjust seasoning if required. Pour half the dressing over the salad and coat.

To serve, place half the salad in a flat serving bowl then layer on the egg, and then add the remaining salad. Drizzle with the remaining dressing and serve immediately.

'Say it with me: nee-SWAHZ.

There's a million takes on this classic out there and I've tried making a lot of them, but this is the version I love the most.

It's easy, healthy, and something the whole family can get into.'

BARBECUE LAMB AND BEETROOT SALAD

SERVES 2

300 g lamb backstrap
250 g asparagus, blanched
40 g rocket
50 g hazelnuts, roasted, peeled and roughly chopped
120 g marinated goat cheese

FOR THE LAMB MARINADE

1 garlic clove
zest and juice of ½ lemon
1 tbsp dried oregano
¼ cup (70 g) Greek yoghurt
big pinch white pepper
big pinch salt flakes
small handful mint leaves
small handful oregano leaves

FOR THE MARINATED BEETROOT

500 g baby beetroot, cooked and peeled
1 tsp raw sugar
1 tsp extra-virgin olive oil
juice of ½ lemon
½ bunch oregano, leaves and stalks finely chopped

Place the lamb backstrap onto a shallow tray.

Combine all the ingredients for the lamb marinade, except the fresh herbs, and blitz with a hand blender. Then pour a quarter of the marinade over the lamb, rub it in, turn the lamb and pour another quarter of the marinade over the lamb. Cover and rest in the fridge for 1–2 hours.

With the rest of the marinade, add the mint and oregano and blitz again until smooth. Set this aside in the fridge for later.

To make the marinated beetroot, cut them in half and put them into a bowl. Add the sugar, salt and pepper, and drizzle with olive oil and mix gently. Let these marinate for as long as you have left to wait for the lamb.

Once the lamb marinade time is up, heat your barbecue or hibachi to high. Cook the lamb until medium rare, about 4 minutes each side, then remove from the heat and allow to rest.

Then add the beetroot onto the grill and cook for a few minutes each side. When they are charred, removed them one at a time and squish them slightly with a potato masher, then put them back onto the grill so the busted up bits get nice and charred.

Return the lamb to the grill for another 2 minutes each side, then remove and carve into slices. I like to go a bit chunkier, closer to 1 cm thick.

Cut the blanched asparagus on a diagonal into roughly 4 cm pieces then place it in a bowl with the carved lamb, rocket and hazelnuts, and drizzle with half of the remaining dressing. Gently fold through the beetroot and goat cheese.

Pour the last bit of the dressing into the bottom of the serving bowl and spread it out evenly with the back of a spoon. Then arrange the salad mix in a loose pile on top and you're ready to serve.

'Beetroot deserves some excitement. What better way to cook it than to whack it on the hibachi for some caramelisation, add in some goat cheese and salad-y things? Then you've got a delicious, hearty (and kiiiiinda healthy) meal to add to your rotation.'

POSH SALADS

ZINGY ZUCCHINI AND PARMESAN SALAD

SERVES 4

4 medium–large zucchini

1 large handful of rocket leaves

1 bunch basil, leaves picked

1 bunch mint, leaves picked

FOR THE DRESSING

juice of 1 large lemon

4½ tbsp (90 ml) extra-virgin olive oil

2 tbsp grated parmesan

Mix the dressing ingredients together and season with salt and pepper. Get the dressing done and off to the side so you're ready to pop this on the table nice and fresh at the last moment. I also find letting it sit gives it a deeper flavour.

Slice the zucchini – you can do this into circles, diagonally or lengthways, just make sure it's super thin (use a mandoline if you have one). Add the zucchini to a bowl with the rest of the salad ingredients, toss through, and season with salt and pepper.

Then dress the zucchini in the mixing bowl – but don't drown it, rather you just want to coat the salad. Pick the dressed salad up with your fingertips and place loosely into the serving bowl so it doesn't sit in a pool of dressing and also is airy and has volume in the bowl, as the zucchini can get dense.

'This is so easy – it's the salad you quickly whip up when you realise you need another side at the last minute.'

Credit: Lauren Zonfrillo

Barbecue
AND
WOODFIRED

BARBECUED EGGPLANT
WITH QUINOA AND BASIL

SERVES 3–4

3 small to medium eggplants
4 tbsp (80 ml) grapeseed oil
20 g finely grated ginger
¼ cup (60 g) doenjang (Korean soybean paste)
2 tsp gochujang (Korean chilli paste)
3 tsp soy sauce
1½ tbsp rice wine vinegar
1½ tsp honey
juice of 1 lime
½ tsp salt
1 lebanese cucumber, roughly chopped
4 spring onions, sliced into matchsticks
¼ cup (50 g) cooked quinoa
¼ bunch basil, leaves picked
¼ bunch mint, leaves picked

Preheat your barbecue grill to high.

Cut your eggplant in half and score the flesh in a diamond pattern – your diamond will be about 1.5 cm x 1.5 cm. Brush with a little bit of oil, season with salt and place skin-side down on the barbecue grill.

Meanwhile, combine the ginger, doenjang, gochujang, soy sauce, rice wine vinegar, honey, lime juice, salt and remaining oil in a bowl and whisk.

Turn your eggplant, and when the flesh side is browning up, flip back to the skin side and brush the ginger mixture on the flesh. Continue to turn and brush the eggplant with the glaze until they are charred and soft, this should take about 4 minutes.

To make the salad topping, combine the cucumber, spring onion, quinoa, basil, mint and a pinch of salt in a bowl and toss lightly. Drizzle the remaining glaze across the bowl and toss.

Remove your eggplants from the grill and put straight onto your platter, then sprinkle the salad mixture over the top and you're ready to serve.

THAI BARBECUE PRAWNS

SERVES 2–3

8 green king prawns

FOR THE NAM JIM-STYLE SAUCE

¼ cup (60 ml) rice wine vinegar

1¼ tbsp palm sugar

2 large makrut lime leaves

10 g lemongrass, sliced

1 tbsp glutinous rice

1 tbsp unsalted peanuts

½ small eschalot, finely chopped

juice and zest of 1 lime

½ birdseye chilli, cut in half lengthways, seeds removed and finely sliced

1¼ tbsp fish sauce

2½ tbsp grapeseed oil

Let's make the sauce first. In a small pot over medium–high heat, combine the rice wine vinegar, palm sugar, makrut leaves and lemongrass and simmer until the liquid has reduced by half. Then strain and discard the solids.

Toast the glutinous rice and peanuts in a dry frying pan over medium heat. Remove and place into a mortar and pestle or bowl, allow it to cool, then grind to a powder. Combine the vinegar mixture and powder with the remaining sauce ingredients in a bowl and stir.

Heat your hibachi or barbecue grill to high.

Use a serrated knife to butterfly the prawns, cutting along the stomach from the head to tail. Carefully remove the vein and discard. Brush the prawns with a little of the sauce and cook on the hibachi or barbecue for 1–2 minutes each side. I like to have a beer at this stage. You don't want to overcook the prawns, but some of the sauce going close to black is very tasty.

Serve straight from the hibachi to a plate, and put any of the remaining sauce on the side for dipping.

Smoking the paperbark at Orana in Residence for the quail dish stuffed with pork, farm greens and kangaroo grass shoyu, in August 2019.
Credit: Nikki To

'When you're cooking over fire, you have to respect the process. It's about patience, about understanding the heat, the timing and the ingredients. There's no rushing it.'

NEGRONI STICKY PORK RIBS

SERVES 4–6

2–3 racks baby back pork ribs (up to 2 kgs – you can marinade them as a rack, or cut them up between the bones)

FOR THE STICKY SAUCE

⅓ cup (90 ml) extra-virgin olive oil

40 g garlic, minced (about 4 cloves)

20 g ginger, minced

400 ml orange or blood orange juice (fresh is best)

1 cup (250 ml) rice wine vinegar

270 ml negroni (equal parts gin, Campari, and sweet vermouth)

scant ¾ cup (160 g) caster sugar

280 g honey

1½ tbsp (30 ml) lemon juice

1½ tbsp (30 ml) Campari

FOR THE MARINADE

40 g garlic, finely chopped or blitzed into a paste in a blender (about 8 cloves)

40 g fresh ginger, finely chopped or blitzed into a paste in a blender

1½ tbsp (30 ml) colatura (if you don't have any of this use white soy or 15 g salt)

1 tsp ground black pepper

1 tsp (60 ml) Campari

zest of 2 oranges (or blood oranges)

Start with your ribs. I always give them a rinse in cold water, then pat them dry with paper towel. Remove that thin membrane underneath – don't skip this. It's the difference between having the meat fall off the bone and not being able to bite through it. Pop them in the fridge uncovered for a half hour or so because dry ribs equals better flavour uptake.

While the ribs are drying in the fridge, start making the sticky sauce. Heat the olive oil in a pan, then add the garlic and ginger. Stir that continuously until they are slightly translucent – when it's about to start caramelising, take it off the heat. This will take about 4 or 5 minutes. Add more olive oil if it starts to dry up.

Add the orange juice, rice wine vinegar, negroni, sugar and honey. Mix and return the pan to a low heat. Let it simmer gently. You're looking for it to reduce by at least half; when it's ready it will coat the back of a spoon. As soon as this happens, turn the heat off and add the lemon juice and Campari to help cool it down.

Now it's time to get onto the marinade. Add all ingredients to a large mixing bowl and stir, then add the ribs and thoroughly mix them into the marinade – get your hands dirty! Leave the ribs in the bowl and cover, then leave them to marinate for as long as you can – a few hours or overnight.

If you have to cook them straight away, which happens to me often, preheat your oven to 180°C and place the ribs onto a tray lined with baking paper. It doesn't matter which side you place them onto the tray as they'll be turned a few times. Add the remaining marinade into the tray as it will add flavour and extra humidity in the oven when they're cooking to keep them tender.

Put your ribs into the oven for about 2 hours. You'll know they're ready when you nudge the meat and it's tender and about to pull away from the bone. You don't want it completely falling off, but as close to that as you can get. If they're not tender, leave them in for another 20 minutes.

When they're ready, take the ribs out of the oven and let them cool for 5–10 minutes. You still want them to be warm when you douse them in the sticky sauce. Gently place the ribs into a bowl and drizzle the sticky sauce all over them to coat them. You can also brush the sticky sauce on, but my preference is dousing. If the sauce is a bit too thick, warm it again for 1–2 minutes on low heat to loosen it up. Coat every single part of the ribs, then place them on a serving plate and you're ready to go!

Credit: Lauren Zonfrillo

WHOLE ROASTED KING DORY

SERVES 2–3

1 whole king dory, head, tail and fins removed

1 cup semi-dried tomatoes

¼ cup baby capers, rinsed

¼ bunch basil, leaves picked and torn

¼ bunch flat-leaf parsley, leaves picked and torn

¼ bunch mint, leaves torn

¼ cup (60 ml) white soy sauce

¼ cup (60 ml) extra-virgin olive oil, plus extra, to drizzle

2 tbsp red wine vinegar

zest and juice of 1 lemon

I always do my whole fish in the woodfired oven, so if you can do that, great. If it's in your conventional oven, preheat it to 220°C.

Score the fish 4–5 times on both sides, using a super sharp knife to cut deeply into the flesh. Don't go all the way to the edge of the fish, stop a couple of centimetres in so the flesh doesn't split when it cooks. Place the fish on a tray and set aside.

Roughly chop half the semi-dried tomatoes and add to a bowl with the remaining whole semi-dried tomatoes, capers and herbs, reserving a spoonful or two for the garnish. Add half the soy sauce, olive oil and vinegar and toss to combine.

Stuff as much of the tomato and herb mixture as possible into the cuts in the fish, drizzle with olive oil and season with salt and pepper. Gently turn the fish and repeat on the other side, then sprinkle with the lemon zest.

Place the fish in the woodfire oven with the thickest end closest to the fire, if in the oven then on the middle rack. Roast until slightly charred, around 15 minutes.

Meanwhile, make up a spray bottle with the remaining oil, soy sauce and vinegar and add half the lemon juice. Check the fish about halfway into the cooking time and spritz with this mixture to slow the caramelisation process and stop the herbs from burning.

When the fish is cooked, remove from the oven and allow to rest for 5 minutes.

Transfer to a platter and pour over any juice that escaped when it was resting. Then squeeze the remaining lemon juice over the top and scatter with the reserved semi-dried tomatoes, capers and herbs.

'It's always best to buy whole fish whenever possible. When roasted in the wood oven with Mediterranean flavours tucked inside, you get all kinds of delicious textures and hidden gems you miss out on with only fillets.'

BARBECUE AND WOODFIRED

PIZZETTA

1 day-old focaccia

extra-virgin olive oil

TOPPING SUGGESTIONS

mortadella

pancetta

pepperoni

mozzarella

scamorza

parmesan

semi-dried tomatoes

cherry tomatoes

roasted capsicum

olives

Preheat a woodfired oven to 300°C or a conventional oven to 180°C.

Slice the focaccia in half lengthways so you have a large piece of focaccia that is about as thick as a pizza base. Drizzle generously with olive oil then toast it up – it will take a couple of minutes in the woodfire or about 15 minutes in the oven.

When it's crispy and starting to toast, it's time to bring it out.

Garnish it with whatever toppings you like and bake for 2–5 minutes so the cheese can melt and slightly brown. This is a good one to do with the kids.

Credit: Lauren Zonfrillo

STUFFED PORCHETTA

SERVES 6–8

1.8 kg–2 kg porchetta (butterflied pork loin with belly attached, bones removed, skin on)

2 tbsp fennel seeds

2½ tsp chilli flakes

½ bunch flat-leaf parsley, roughly chopped

small bunch oregano, roughly chopped

small bunch sage, roughly chopped

4 smoked garlic cloves, roughly chopped

zest and juice of 1 lemon

1½ tbsp extra-virgin olive oil

1½ tbsp salt

1 tsp white pepper

grapeseed oil, for rubbing

Pat your pork dry thoroughly with paper towel then prick holes across the surface of the skin – I have a belly skin crisping tool and meat tenderiser that has lots of spikes coming out of it to make the process easier.

In a dry pan over medium heat, toast the fennel seeds and chilli flakes until aromatic, tip into a mortar and pestle and let it cool. Add in the herbs, smoked garlic, lemon zest and olive oil and pound together to make a rough paste.

Rub the inside of the pork thoroughly with 1 tablespoon of salt and the white pepper, then spread the rough paste evenly across the flesh.

Then tightly roll the porchetta using butcher's twine to tie it at regular intervals. Wipe off any parts that are bursting out the side, pat the skin dry with paper towel, and place on a plate or an open container in the fridge overnight.

The next day remove the pork from the fridge and pat it dry, it's best if it comes to room temperature before cooking but not a disaster if you don't have the time.

Preheat your woodfired oven to 240°C or a conventional oven to 120°C. Put in the pork and roast for 1 hour in the woodfired oven or 2 hours in the conventional oven. When the core temperature reaches 40°C remove it from the oven.

If you're using a conventional oven, increase the temperature to 240°C so it can heat up while you're doing this next step.

Rub the pork skin with lemon juice, grapeseed oil and the remaining salt. Roast for another 20–30 minutes to allow the skin to crackle, then remove from the oven when the core temperature reaches 50°C. Rest for 30 minutes – the core temperature will keep increasing and will hit 60°C. Remove the string and carve – sometimes a serrated knife is the best way of cleanly getting through the crackling.

WOODFIRED SCALLOPS
WITH JALAPEÑO AND LIME

SERVES 2–3

12 live scallops
extra-virgin olive oil, to drizzle

FOR THE SAUCE

1 tbsp rice wine vinegar
zest of 1 lime
juice of 2 limes
2 tbsp green olive brine
2–4 tsp jalapeño hot sauce, to taste
1½ tbsp extra-virgin olive oil
white soy sauce, to taste
¼ bunch mint, finely sliced
¼ bunch flat-leaf parsley, finely sliced
¼ bunch coriander, finely sliced

Preheat your woodfired oven to 300°C or conventional oven to as high as it goes.

If you need to shuck your scallops (which is my preference), insert a small palette knife into the hinge and separate the scallop's adductor muscle from where it joins the top of the shell. With the shell now open, cut the black gut sack from the white meat and remove it along with the frill. Run a spoon hard against the bottom of the shell to slide under the scallop and remove it completely from the shell. Repeat with the remaining scallops.

Wash the scallops (just the meat, not the shell) thoroughly in cold salted water – I use cold water and add 3% salt, but you can be a bit more abstract and add in a teaspoon to a bowl. Remove the veins (aka poo chutes) and place on paper towel to dry.

Wash and dry the bottom shells thoroughly and place on a baking tray. Place the scallops in a bowl and drizzle with a touch of olive oil, season with salt and white pepper, then place each scallop on a dry shell. Roast for 1 minute (no longer!) Remove the scallops from the shells and set aside.

Combine all the ingredients for the sauce in a bowl, mix well and add the scallops back in, mixing gently to ensure each scallop is covered beautifully. Place a spoonful of the herbs from the sauce in the bottom of each shell, followed by a scallop, and then another spoonful of sauce. Roast for 1 more minute, then serve straight away.

'Don't be scared of fresh scallops – they are super simple to prepare and I guarantee they're a crowd-pleaser. This version is one of my favourite quick bites to do in the wood oven, with jalapeño for a bit of bite and fresh lime and herbs to brighten it up.'

Jock camping out near Daly River, Northern Territory, in July 2014.
Credit: Per-Anders Jörgensen

'One of the main lessons I've learnt is to give back more than you take, and that has become a core part of my life.'

SPICY PORK SKEWERS
WITH SUMMER CHOPPED SALAD

SERVES 4

800 g pork neck

FOR THE PORK MARINADE

1 bunch flat-leaf parsley

1 bunch spring onions, green part only (reserve the white part for salad)

½ cup (100 g) pickled jalapeño

5 tbsp (50 g) anchovies

2½ tbsp capers

zest and juice of 1 lemon

2½ tbsp extra-virgin olive oil

1½ tbsp red wine vinegar

½ tbsp white soy sauce

FOR THE SUMMER CHOPPED SALAD

3 corn cobs, husk on

extra-virgin olive oil, to drizzle

2 avocados, chopped

1 lebanese cucumber, chopped

1 head cos lettuce or treviso radicchio, chopped

reserved spring onions, white part only, chopped

First, we marinade. Slice the pork neck into 1 cm-thick slices, then cut each slice in half lengthways.

Place all the marinade ingredients in a blender and blitz until smooth. Pour half of the marinade over the pork (keep the rest for dressing the salad). Massage the marinade into the meat thoroughly, then cover and pop it in the fridge for at least 30 minutes.

If you're making your own pita bread – which is my preference, but no judgement if you grab some from the shops – this is the moment to start.

Tip the flour and yeast into a large mixing bowl and combine. Pour in the warm water, salt and olive oil, then mix it all together with your hand, a wooden spoon, or in a stand mixer with a dough hook. Once it starts coming together into a rough dough, keep going until it forms a shaggy, slightly sticky ball.

Turn it out onto a clean bench – no extra flour needed unless it's really sticky – and knead it for 8–10 minutes until smooth and springy. It should bounce back when you give it a gentle prod.

Pop the dough into a lightly oiled bowl, cover with a clean damp tea towel or cling film, and leave it in a warm spot until doubled in size – about an hour.

Once it's puffed up, knock the air out and divide into 8 even pieces. Roll each one into a ball and rest under a tea towel for 10 minutes. This helps relax the gluten so they're easier to shape. Then roll each piece out into a circle about 4 mm thick – not too thin, not too thick. Even thickness means a better puff when cooking.

Preheat a heavy pan or cast-iron skillet over medium–high heat (or fire up the wood oven if you've got one). Cook each pita for 1–2 minutes on each side. They should puff up into gorgeous little pillows. Wrap the cooked pittas in a clean tea towel to keep them soft and warm.

If you're cooking your corn in the oven, preheat to 250°C now. While the dough is rising or the pork is marinating, get started on the salad.

Peel back the husks of the corn – don't remove them fully – and season the cobs with salt and a drizzle of extra-virgin olive oil. Fold the husks back over and place the corn in an ovenproof dish with a splash of water. Turn the husks to moisten all over, then roast in the oven until the husks are charred and the kernels are tender and sweet.

FOR THE PITA BREAD

500 g plain flour	
7 g instant dried yeast	
335 g warm water	
10 g salt	
1 tsp extra-virgin olive oil	

(If you're in a rush, microwave the corn in the husks for about 5 minutes. Or strip the husks and chuck the cobs straight on the barbecue for 10 minutes or so.)

Once the corn is cooked, cut the kernels from the cob, let them cool slightly, then mix with the rest of the salad ingredients in a big bowl. Add the reserved marinade and toss gently.

When you're ready to cook, preheat your barbecue. While that's heating up, thread the marinated pork onto metal skewers.

Grill the skewers, letting each side char nicely. Remove them from the heat once the internal temp hits 60°C, then rest for 5 minutes.

Carve the pork skewer directly into the salad and mix through. Then serve on the table with the warm pita bread – I like to rip open one end and fill my pita up, but you decide.

ANCHOVY AND GUANCIALE TOAST

SERVES 6–8

1 white sourdough loaf

extra-virgin olive oil

white anchovies

guanciale (Italian cured pork)

anchovies in oil

pepper

OPTIONAL

tomato paste

chilli, finely chopped

pesto

garlic cloves

Preheat a woodfired oven to 300°C or an oven grill to 250°C.

Slice your sourdough into 3 cm slices. Remove crusts and cut into fat fingers.

Arrange on a baking tray and drizzle with olive oil on all sides. Toast lightly under the grill or in the woodfired oven until evenly coloured on all sides.

Place two white anchovies on a piece of toast followed by a guanciale slice over the top. Repeat on the other toasts, alternating anchovies in oil and white anchovies.

For variety, you could also spread the toast with a little tomato paste mixed with finely chopped chilli or pesto, or rub a garlic clove over the toast. Place anchovies and guanciale over the top.

Arrange the anchovy and guanciale-topped toast on a baking tray and place in the oven or under the grill for 10–30 seconds, rotating until the guanciale is translucent. Arrange on a serving platter and season with pepper – happy days!

DESSERTS

SUMMER FRUIT CRUMBLE
WITH COCONUT ICE CREAM

SERVES 6–8

FOR THE COCONUT ICE CREAM

⅓ cup (100 g) glucose

⅓ cup plus 1 tbsp (100 g) caster sugar

½ cup (125 ml) coconut water

4 cups (1 litre) coconut cream

2 g xanthan gum

pinch of salt

FOR THE BERRY FILLING

200 g each raspberries, blueberries and blackberries

100 g strawberries, hulled and roughly chopped

2 tbsp raw caster sugar

3 tsp cornflour

zest and juice of 1 lemon

3 tsp red wine vinegar

pinch of salt

FOR THE CRUMBLE

1⅔ cups (160 g) moist coconut flakes

½ cup (110 g) raw caster sugar

1½ cups (225 g) plain flour

¾ tsp baking powder

pinch of salt

190 g unsalted butter, frozen

2 egg yolks

Preheat the oven to 180°C and line a baking tray with baking paper. Grease a 21 cm pie dish.

To make the coconut ice cream, dissolve the glucose, sugar and coconut water in a saucepan over medium heat. Mix in the coconut cream. Add xanthan gum and salt, then blend with a stick blender to fully incorporate. Churn in an ice cream maker until set, about 30 minutes, then store in the freezer until ready to serve.

Combine all the ingredients for the berry filling in a bowl and leave to macerate.

Combine the dry ingredients for the crumble in a large bowl. Grate in the frozen butter and rub into the mixture with the egg yolks. Place half of the crumble mixture on the prepared baking tray and bake for about 5 minutes until golden, then pack tightly into the bottom of the prepared pie dish.

Add the macerated berry filling to the pie dish, then cover with the remaining raw crumble. Bake in the oven for about 30 minutes – you will know it's cooked when the crumble is golden and the berry filling will be bubbling hot out the sides.

Leave to cool for 5 minutes before serving with the coconut ice cream.

'This is the crumble of my dreams – serve with a HUUUGE scoop of vegan coconut ice cream!'

TORTA CAPRESE

SERVES 8–10

250 g dark chocolate

250 g almonds, skin on

250 g butter, room temperature and cut into cubes

170 g white sugar

5 eggs, separated

Preheat the oven to 180°C.

Butter the base and sides of a 23 cm springform pan, then dust with flour and set aside.

Coarsely chop up the chocolate and set aside. Place the almonds into a food processor and blitz to a rough crumble and set aside.

Add the butter into your mixer and turn onto medium speed for 1 minute. With the mixer still on, add your sugar gradually until they are combined. If it sticks to the side, stop your blender and scrap down the sides, and then switch it back on. Separate your eggs (reserving the egg whites for later), and add the egg yolk into the mixer (which is still turned on) and keep mixing for 2 minutes.

Add your dark chocolate and mix on high for a few minutes. Then add the almonds and mix on medium for a few more minutes. Keep scrapping down the sides if it looks like the mix is creeping up. It should now be really thick and look like a thick almond chocolate paste.

Whip the egg whites into medium to firm peaks, then fold into the almond chocolate mixture.

Pour the mixture into the cake tin – spread it evenly and then tap the cake tin firmly on the bench two or three times to do a final level. Put into the oven for 38 minutes.

When the cake has cooled, turn out upside down onto a wire rack, then turn up the right way onto the serving plate. Serve with whipped cream or ice cream.

'We met Shirley in Puglia and, after I ate a few of these tortas, she agreed to show me how to make them.'

JOCK'S APPLE TARTE TATIN

SERVES 6–8

5–8 pink lady apples

150 g unsalted butter

scant 1 cup (200 g) raw sugar

1 vanilla pod, seeds scraped and pods roughly chopped

2 whole star anise

generous pinch of salt flakes

1½ tsp black peppercorns, crushed

1 sheet puff pastry

¼ cup (60 ml) apple juice (from apple trimmings or store-bought, see Note)

vanilla ice cream, to serve

Preheat the oven to 220°C.

Peel the apples, then cut in half vertically. Trim the tops and tails to create even-sized, centre-cut apple slices and use a melon baller to remove the core.

If you're making your own apple juice, juice the scraps of the apples and reserve for the caramel sauce.

Place an ovenproof 20 cm-diameter saucepan with 6 cm sides over medium–high heat. You need these sides to be at a 9 degree angle, a high edged normal frying pan won't give you the edge you need. To make the caramel sauce, add the butter; once it begins to melt, add sugar, vanilla, star anise, salt and pepper. Cook, stirring often, until golden brown then remove from heat.

Pour half of the caramel into another pan, then arrange the apple halves around the ovenproof pan, packing them in tightly so they completely cover the base of the pan.

Trim your puff pastry into a 24 cm circle, then place on top of the apples and tuck the excess down the sides of the pan with a knife. Use a sharp knife to score a few holes into the pastry, then put into the oven and bake for 40 minutes or until the pastry is deeply golden.

Meanwhile, add the apple juice to the remaining caramel. Bring to a simmer over medium heat and cook until the caramel is deeply golden, thick and glossy. Strain through a fine sieve into a jug.

When the tarte is cooked, place a large plate, upside down, over the saucepan. Quickly and carefully flip the saucepan and plate over as one to turn the tarte onto the plate, and serve with vanilla ice cream and the jug of caramel sauce.

NOTE: *If using store-bought apple juice, opt for cold-pressed, cloudy apple juice. And at Christmas time, I jam Christmas pudding inbetween the apple halves before I put the pastry on.*

'I promise it's not that hard to make. I even bought the pastry from the supermarket to make it simpler!'

BANANA BREAD WITH ALFIE

SERVES 8

- 280 g jaggery (unrefined sugar), roughly chopped
- 60 g unsalted butter
- 4 super-ripe bananas (about 460 g), peeled
- 2 eggs
- ⅓ cup (90 g) Greek yoghurt
- 2½ tsp baking powder
- ½ tsp salt
- 1¾ cups (280 g) plain flour

Preheat the oven to 170°C. Grease and line a deep loaf tin (24 x 13 x 6.5 cm) with baking paper.

Place the jaggery in a pan with the butter over medium heat. Cook until it turns into emulsified toffee goodness.

Meanwhile, place the bananas in a large bowl and mash, taking care not to turn it into a puree – you want some lumps in there! Pour the sugar and butter mixture into the banana and mix well. Crack in the eggs and whisk until fully incorporated.

Mix in the yoghurt, baking powder and salt, then add the flour and mix well. Pour the mixture into the prepared loaf tin and bake for 1 hour, turning halfway to ensure it browns evenly.

Leave to cool before slicing and serving.

BLOOD ORANGE AND NEGRONI CAKE

SERVES 10–12

8 blood oranges
200 g unsalted butter
1⅓ cups (300 g) raw caster sugar
3 eggs
¾ cup (200 g) Greek yoghurt
¾ cup (130 g) fine semolina
¾ cup (100 g) plain flour
heaped ¾ cup (100 g) almond meal
3 tsp cream of tartar
1 tsp baking soda
pinch of salt

FOR THE NEGRONI SYRUP AND CREAM SWIRL

¾ cup plus 1 tbsp (200 ml) Campari
5 tbsp (100 ml) gin
5 tbsp (100 ml) sweet vermouth
1⅓ cups (300 g) raw caster sugar
¾ cup plus 1 tbsp (200 ml) thickened cream

Preheat the oven to 160°C and line a 25 cm springform cake tin with baking paper.

Cut 2 blood oranges into 5 mm rounds. Zest and juice the remaining 6 oranges. Strain the orange juice to remove the pulp.

To make the syrup, in a medium saucepan, combine the Campari, gin, vermouth, sugar and orange juice and bring to a boil. Skim any impurities and reduce the heat to a simmer. Add orange slices and simmer until softened (about 5 minutes), turning them halfway. Carefully remove the slices and continue simmering the negroni syrup until reduced by half. Meanwhile, cover the bottom of the cake tin with the candied orange slices.

To make the cake batter, place the butter and sugar in a saucepan over medium heat to melt the butter while whisking to emulsify. Transfer to a mixing bowl and leave to cool slightly. Whisk in the eggs one at a time, then whisk in the yoghurt and orange zest.

Combine the dry ingredients in a separate bowl and fold into the wet mixture. Pour the batter into the prepared cake tin and bake, rotating halfway, for 1 hour or until a wooden skewer inserted into the centre of the cake comes out clean.

Once the cake is cooled, turn it out onto a serving plate with the orange slices facing up and use the blunt end of a skewer to prick multiple holes across the top of the cake. Pour over half of the negroni syrup, then prick more holes. Leave to soak for 20 minutes.

Whip the cream to soft peaks then fold through the remaining negroni syrup to create a swirl effect. Spoon the negroni swirl on the sliced cake to serve.

'I'm not much of a cake guy but, being a massive negroni fan, I'd grab a slice of this any time of day.'

DESSERTS

CARROT CAKE

SERVES 8–10

3 egg yolks
heaped ¾ cup (180 g) tightly packed brown sugar
¼ cup (30 g) roughly chopped walnuts
⅓ cup (60 g) raisins
1 large carrot (about 130 g), peeled and coarsely grated
1 cup (150 g) plain flour
¾ tsp ground cinnamon
¾ tsp bicarbonate of soda
¾ tsp baking powder
5 tbsp (100 ml) grapeseed oil

FOR THE CREAM CHEESE ICING

500 g cream cheese, softened
140 g unsalted butter, softened
heaped ½ cup (100 g) icing sugar, sifted
1 tbsp honey
1 tsp vanilla paste
1 tbsp lemon juice

FOR THE CANDIED CARROT

2 baby carrots (or 1 large carrot)
1 cup (225 g) caster sugar
1 cup (250 ml) water

Preheat the oven to 160°C and line a 21 cm springform cake tin with baking paper.

In the bowl of a stand mixer fitted with a whisk, combine the egg yolks and sugar and beat on high speed until pale and thick enough that the mixture falls in ribbons from the whisk (about 5 minutes).

Remove the bowl from the mixer and fold in the walnuts, raisins and carrot by hand. In another bowl, whisk all the dry ingredients until combined, then gently fold into the egg mixture. Gradually pour in the grapeseed oil and continue to fold.

Pour the batter into the prepared cake tin and bake, rotating halfway, for 1 hour or until a wooden skewer inserted into the centre of the cake comes out clean. Allow the cake to cool to room temperature before icing.

For the cream cheese icing, combine all ingredients in a bowl with a spatula or in a stand mixer fitted with a paddle attachment. Pass through a fine sieve if you wish to ensure it is extra smooth.

For the candied carrot, use a mandoline or vegetable peeler to slice the carrot lengthways as thinly as possible. (If using a large carrot, cut each slice in half lengthways with a knife.)

Dissolve the sugar and water in a pot over medium heat, then add carrot and simmer until tender and translucent (about 15 minutes). Strain.

Line an oven tray with baking paper and lightly spray the surface with baking spray. Place carrot strips on the tray and bake at 100°C for 20 minutes. Remove the strips from the oven and, working one at a time, coil tightly around a chopstick. Allow to stand until the coil shape sets, then carefully remove from the chopstick. Leave to cool fully at room temperature until crisp (about 30 minutes).

To assemble, slice the cooled cake in half horizontally through the centre. Spread half the icing on the bottom layer, cover with the top layer of cake and cover the top with the remaining icing. Top with as many candied carrot coils as you possibly can!

Jock making his paperbark ice cream on a *MasterChef Australia* Masterclass, in May 2022.
Credit: Endemol Shine Australia

'There is nothing I'm more frightened of in life than doing something badly, and so cooking in front of a television audience of millions was not top of the pops for me.'

TRADITIONAL SCOTTISH SHORTBREAD

MAKES 3

420 g unsalted butter, softened

¾ cup (180 g) caster sugar

4 cups (600 g) plain flour, plus extra, for dusting

Preheat the oven to 150°C and line a baking tray with baking paper.

Using a stand mixer fitted with a paddle attachment, beat the butter and sugar together on medium speed. Turn off the mixer. Add flour, turn the mixer speed to low and mix until the dough is just combined.

Turn the dough out onto a clean work surface and bring together with your hands. If using a wooden shortbread mould, portion dough into appropriate sizes (this recipe is enough for 3 x 200 g pieces) and use your hands to pat it into a rough shape slightly larger than the mould, or form into 18 cm rounds, crimp the edges and cut into triangles.

Use a pastry brush to thoroughly coat the inside of the mould, and the top surface of the dough, with plain flour. Press the dough into the mould, then trim off the excess with a knife. Carefully transfer to the prepared baking tray.

Bake for 30 minutes or until light blond in colour. Allow to cool fully on the tray before serving.

NOTE: *If you don't have a shortbread mould, divide into three portions and form the dough into your preferred shape with your hands. Take care not to overwork the dough.*

'There's a reason this classic has stuck through the ages. It's incredibly easy but also uses a heap of BUTTER.'

LEMON DRIZZLE CAKE

SERVES 8–10

200 g unsalted butter, chopped, at room temperature

1 cup (225 g) caster sugar

zest and juice of 3 lemons

3 eggs, at room temperature

1¼ cups (200 g) plain flour

1 tsp baking powder

¼ tsp salt

½ cup (110 g) raw sugar

Preheat the oven to 160°C and grease and line a 24 cm x 13 cm x 6.5 cm loaf tin.

Beat the butter, caster sugar and lemon zest together in a bowl until light and fluffy. Add eggs, one at a time, beating after each addition. Add the juice of 1 lemon and stir to combine.

In another large bowl, whisk together the flour, baking powder and salt, then fold into the butter mixture.

Pour the batter into the prepared loaf tin and bake, rotating halfway, for 50–60 minutes or until a wooden skewer inserted into the centre of the cake comes out clean.

Combine the remaining lemon juice and the raw sugar. Pour over the warm cake while still in the tin, then leave to cool.

ALMOND CANTUCCI

MAKES 12

2 cups (300 g) plain flour
1 cup (225 g) caster sugar
1 tsp baking powder
zest of 1 orange
zest of 2 lemons
2 eggs
½ tsp vanilla extract, use paste if you can find it
125 g whole blanched almonds

Preheat your oven to 180°C and line a baking tray with baking paper.

Add the flour, sugar and baking powder into a mixing bowl, and give it a good mix through. Zest in your citrus – all of it. If you've got a blood orange kicking around, swap it for the orange. If you're playing around with pistachios or hazelnuts instead, flip it and go heavy on the orange and light on the lemon.

Make a well in the centre and crack in your eggs and vanilla. Give it a gentle whisk with a fork, then start folding the flour mix in. When it starts to come together and lose its stick, get your hands in there. That's when the real dough begins. Knead it for a few minutes until it just turns tacky again – don't skip this or you'll end up with a tight texture in what are already dense biscuits.

Add in your almonds and work them through the dough with your hands. And that is it, so simple.

Split the dough in two. Wet your hands (this part's messy) and shape each half into a rustic log, about 25 cm long. Place them on your tray – they'll puff out, so give them room.

Bake for 30 minutes, then let them cool on the tray for 10 minutes. While still a bit warm, slice them into 1 cm-thick fingers with a serrated knife. Turn them on their sides and return to the oven for another few minutes to dry out and get that golden snap.

Now you're ready to dunk. I'm partial to a Sommelier's Breakfast – espresso with a cheeky shot of Campari – but these work just as well with a cuppa.

'Cantucci and biscotti ... same thing.'

CAMPARI CASSATELLE

MAKES 20

2¼ cups (340 g) plain flour

1½ tbsp raw caster sugar

zest of 1 blood orange

pinch of salt

30 g unsalted butter, melted

1 shot (30 ml) Campari

2 eggs, whisked

2 tbsp water

vegetable oil, for deep frying

icing sugar, for dusting

whipped cream, to serve

FOR THE FILLING

½ cup (110 g) caster sugar

zest of 1 blood orange

1 tbsp blood orange juice

1 tsp vanilla extract

½ tbsp honey

pinch of salt

1 shot (30 ml) Campari

⅔ cup (75 g) almond meal

200 g ricotta, drained (see Note)

To make the pastry, sift the flour in a medium-sized bowl and whisk in the sugar, zest and salt. Form a well in the centre and add the butter, Campari and eggs. Use a wooden spoon to mix together, gradually adding the water until it forms a cohesive mass. Tip out onto a clean work surface and knead the dough for about 2 minutes until it is smooth and soft. Transfer to a bowl and cover with a plate. Set aside to rest for 30 minutes.

To make the filling, place sugar, zest, juice, vanilla extract, honey and salt in a saucepan over medium heat and reduce until syrupy. Add Campari and almond meal and bring back to a boil. Remove from heat then stir through ricotta and leave to cool.

Cut the dough in half, then roll out one half on a lightly floured work surface to 2 mm thick. Cut out circles of dough using a 9 cm round cookie cutter. Place 1 heaped teaspoon of the ricotta filling on each circle and lightly run your finger, dipped in water, around the rim. Fold the circle of dough in half, enclosing the ricotta filling. Place the soft edge of the 5 cm cookie cutter directly over the filling bulge and press gently. Using the 7 cm sharp edge of the cookie cutter, encompass the whole cassatelle and cut the remaining dough. You should be left with a neat dough formation that has a small amount of dough outlining the filling. Place on a lightly floured baking tray and repeat with the remaining dough and filling.

Fill a heavy-based pot no more than halfway with vegetable oil and heat to 170°C or until a scrap of dough dropped into the oil bubbles immediately. Cook the cassatelle in batches of 2–3 for 3–4 minutes, turning halfway, until golden brown all over. Drain on paper towel and set aside to cool slightly. Dust with icing sugar and serve warm, with whipped cream if desired.

NOTE: *It's best to use drained ricotta for this recipe – the drier the ricotta, the better! To drain, place the ricotta in a sieve or muslin cloth over a bowl in the refrigerator overnight before making the filling.*

Jock in Bologna, Italy with Alfie and Isla, August 2022.
Credit: Lauren Zonfrillo

BUMBLE BEES

MAKES 6

100 g dark chocolate

1 cup (90 g) moist coconut flakes

⅓ cup (75 ml) sweetened condensed milk

2 pieces dried mango

12 flaked almonds

Preheat the oven to 180°C and line a baking tray with baking paper.

Chop 15 g of the chocolate into small pieces and combine with the coconut flakes and condensed milk in a bowl. Mix, then portion into 25 g balls to form the bumble bee bodies. Press into firm spheres and place on the prepared baking tray. Bake for 8–9 minutes.

Meanwhile, melt the remaining chocolate in a heatproof bowl over a saucepan of simmering water. Place the mango slices in a small bowl and cover with hot water. Once they've softened up, pat dry and cut into thin strips.

To assemble the bumble bees, dip the top half of the bee body into the melted chocolate, shake off any excess, and place on a wire rack.

Wrap three mango strips around the body of each bee to create stripes. Stick two almond flakes into each bumble bee's back to make their wings, and you're ready to go!

SUMMER BERRIES
WITH GREEK YOGHURT AND PISTACHIO PRALINE

SERVES 2

2 punnets summer berries, such as raspberries and blueberries

4 tbsp Greek yoghurt, whipped cream, or an equal mix of both

FOR THE PISTACHIO PRALINE

½ cup (70 g) pistachios, shelled

1 cup (225g) sugar

2 cups (500 ml) water

Preheat the oven to 180°C and line a baking tray with baking paper.

Roast the pistachios on a different baking tray for a few minutes, or dry toast on the stove in a saucepan over medium heat. Keep an eye on them, as they will burn in an instant!

Pour the toasted pistachios onto the lined baking tray and space out evenly.

Place the sugar and water in a small pot over low heat. Do an initial stir when you add the ingredients then don't stir the mixture again. When it turns a deep golden colour, which should take around 25 minutes, carefully pour it evenly over the pistachios. It will be as hot as lava, so don't put your finger in it! Give the tray a little shoogle so that everything is as even and flat as possible.

Set aside, and when it's completely cool, it will be hard enough to break into shards or small pieces.

To build the dessert, divide the berries into tumblers or wine glasses, making sure the better-looking berries are around the sides of the glass. Spoon 2 heaped dessert spoons of the Greek yoghurt or whipped cream into each glass. There's no need to flatten it out or make this pretty, but it will look better if the yoghurt/cream doesn't touch the sides of the glass, so try to place it in the centre of the berries.

Top with the praline. If serving to adults only, break the praline into large shards so it can be used to scoop out the berries. If it's for kids, bash or blitz the praline into a fine powder.

NOTE: *The praline will keep in a sealed glass jar for at least a month.*

Recipes JOCK NICKED

'If you're going to nick a recipe, nick it from the best,' Jock would say with a grin – and that's exactly what he did. These are the recipes he lifted from the pages of his mates' cookbooks and cooked so often they started to feel like his own. He didn't rewrite them. He didn't need to. He just cooked the hell out of them, over and over, for the people he loved.

STUFFED ROASTED SALMON
WITH JERSEY ROYALS, SPRING ASPARAGUS AND WILD GARLIC PESTO
— JAMIE OLIVER —

SERVES 12

olive oil

1 bunch of mint (30 g)

1 fresh red chilli

1 handful of wild garlic

1 lemon

1 bunch of asparagus (350 g)

1 large handful of breadcrumbs

2 kg Jersey Royal new potatoes (or use another new potato variety – kipfler, dutch cream or sebago)

2 x 1.2 kg sides of salmon, scaled and pin-boned, from sustainable sources

8 slices of higher-welfare prosciutto

1 bunch of thyme (20 g), ideally the flowering kind

FOR THE PESTO

1 handful of wild garlic

1 bunch of flat-leaf parsley (30 g)

50 g blanched almonds

50 g cheddar or parmesan cheese, or a mixture of the two

extra-virgin olive oil

Jersey Royals are one of the heroes of springtime, and need to be embraced when you see them. I'm making double use of a deliciously optimistic wild garlic pesto, both as a dressing for the spuds and as part of an epic stuffing for this showstopper roasted salmon. It looks super-fancy, but is actually straightforward to put together, perfect for a celebration meal with people you love.

Preheat the oven to 220°C. To make a stuffing for the fish, put a large non-stick frying pan on a medium-high heat with 2 tablespoons of olive oil. Pick in the mint leaves, reserving the stalks, then finely slice and add the chilli. Tear in the wild garlic leaves, with any flowers, and finely grate in the lemon zest.

Snap the woody ends off the asparagus and finely slice the stalks, leaving the tips whole. Add it all to the pan to cook for a couple of minutes – remember it will continue to cook inside the salmon later.

Season the mixture with sea salt and black pepper, toss in the breadcrumbs, tip onto a board and leave to cool.

For the pesto, tear the wild garlic leaves and parsley into a pestle and mortar with a pinch of salt, and pound into a paste. Bash in the nuts, finely grate in the cheese, and muddle in about 3 tablespoons of extra-virgin olive oil to give you a spoonable pesto. Now, I like to finish it with just a little squeeze of lemon juice, which isn't traditional, but cuts through nicely.

Season the flesh side of each side of salmon with salt and pepper, then spread 2 tablespoons of pesto across each.

Lay out 7 pieces of string (about 30 cm in length), about 4 cm apart, and sit one of the salmon sides on top, skin-side down. Spoon over the filling and pat and press it all over the salmon, then sit the other side on top, pesto-side down.

Continued overleaf >

Credit: © Jamie Oliver Enterprises Ltd, 2023, by Chris Terry

Lay over the prosciutto slices, then drizzle the bunch of thyme with oil and scatter the sprigs over the salmon. Tie the pieces of string together around the salmon, securing everything in place.

Slice the remaining lemon, and arrange in a large greaseproof paper-lined tray, then sit the stuffed salmon on top. Place in the oven, then immediately reduce the temperature to 180°C, and roast for 35 minutes, or until beautifully cooked through.

Put the mint stalks into a large pan of salted boiling water, then add the potatoes, halving any larger ones. Cook for 10 to 15 minutes, or until tender, then turn the heat off and leave them to steep in that lovely mint water.

Remove the salmon from the oven and baste with the juices in the tray. Let it rest for 10 minutes, then remove the string and the thyme.

Drain the potatoes, discard the mint stalks and – while the potatoes are still hot and steaming – dress with the remaining pesto.

Slice the salmon, and serve with the pesto-dressed potatoes and a simple seasonal salad.

EASY SWAPS

- If you can't get hold of wild garlic, you can swap a bunch of fresh flat-leaf parsley into your stuffing mix, and replace it with any soft herb you fancy for the pesto: think basil, mint, rocket or simply double parsley.

- I've used almonds for the pesto, but feel free to swap in what you've got – hazelnuts, pistachios or pine nuts would all work a treat.

KITCHEN KIT

- No pestle and mortar? No problem! You can absolutely make the pesto in a blender or food processor, you'll just get a slightly smoother texture than the rustic one you get from a pestle and mortar.

GET AHEAD

- If you want to be ahead of the game, you can prep the stuffed salmon the day before, then cover and keep in the fridge overnight. Just get it out an hour before you want to cook, so you're not cooking it from super cold.

Recipe © Jamie Oliver Enterprises Limited, 2024. Photography: © Jamie Oliver Enterprises Ltd, 2023, by Chris Terry.

CHICKEN LIVER PARFAIT
— MARCO PIERRE WHITE —

SERVES 4

3 shallots, sliced
1 small clove garlic
thyme
100 ml brandy
100 ml port
100 ml Madeira
250 g chicken or duck livers, cleaned
750 g unsalted butter
5 large eggs
1 tsp sel rose
1 tsp salt
¼ tsp white pepper

Place the shallots, garlic, thyme, brandy, port and Madeira in a small saucepan. Bring to a gentle simmer and let it bubble away until it's reduced to a rich, syrupy consistency – you're after a glaze that coats the back of a spoon.

Pour this hot syrup over the chicken livers, give it a stir, and vacuum seal the lot together. (No sealer? A sturdy ziplock with the air squeezed out will do.) Vacuum seal the butter separately.

Warm both the liver mix and butter in a water bath set to 60°C. You're not cooking them yet, just gently bringing everything up to temperature.

Once warm, pop the livers and their juices into a Thermomix or blender and blitz until smooth. While the motor's running, slowly add the eggs, one at a time, giving each one a chance to fully blend in before adding the next.

Pass the mixture through a superbag or fine sieve into a bowl sitting over hot tap water. This keeps it loose and ready to take the butter.

Using a stick blender, slowly emulsify the warm melted butter into the liver mixture. Season with the sel rose, salt and white pepper. Take your time here – it should look impossibly silky.

Pour the parfait into a 32-cm stoneware rectangular terrine mould. Cover with foil, smoothing the top so there are no air pockets. Cover tightly with more foil.

Place the mould into a bain-marie (deep roasting tray half-filled with hot water) and bake at 90°C for around 45 minutes. Check by giving it a gentle wobble – the parfait should move as one, like a set custard.

As soon as it's done, whip it out of the oven and cool it straight away in the fridge. Let it set completely before slicing.

Don't overcomplicate how you serve this. It's great with some crackers, slices of fresh baguette, or toasted brioche.

FERMENTED CHILLI GLAZED CHICKEN
— ANDY ALLEN —

SERVES 6

200 g fermented chilli sauce

1 medium-sized free-range chicken

FOR THE FERMENTED CHILLI SAUCE

20 fermented red chillies (see instructions)

330 ml apple cider vinegar

4 garlic cloves

120 ml vegetable oil

30 g ginger

80 g brown sugar

1 tbsp cooking salt

To ferment the red chillies, place in a jar and submerge in a 5% salt brine. Whack the lid on the jar and place in a warm place for 7–10 days. Every two days, open and close the lid to release the build-up of gases.

Once the chillies have fermented, drain them to remove the brine and place the chillies along with all of the other chilli sauce ingredients into a blender. Blend for 2 minutes on high, until the sauce is smooth.

Preheat your oven to 240°C.

Butterfly the chicken by removing the backbone and wishbone, then press flat on a roasting pan, skin side up. Brush both sides of the chicken with about half of the chilli sauce and season well with salt.

Place the chicken in the oven for 25–30 minutes, or until the internal temperature reaches 60°C. Throughout the cooking time, brush the chicken 4–5 times with more of the chilli sauce.

The chicken should be bright red, charred and sticky. Serve with a couple of fresh lemon cheeks.

Credit: Jock Zonfrillo

SEA BREAM WITH TOMATO AND HERB SALSA
— GORDON RAMSAY —

SERVES 4

olive oil, for frying

2 sea bream fillets, about 150 g each

FOR THE TOMATO AND HERB SALSA

olive oil

200 g cherry tomatoes

60 g pitted black olives (Kalamata if possible), drained

small bunch of coriander

small bunch of basil

1 lemon

sea salt and freshly ground black pepper

First make the salsa. Place a small saucepan over a gentle heat and add 3 tablespoons of olive oil. Chop the tomatoes in half and add to the oil. Add the olives, season with salt and pepper and stir over a low heat for 1–2 minutes. Set aside.

Hold the coriander and basil stalks together and slice down with a sharp knife to shave off the leaves. Discard the stalks, then gently roll the coriander and basil leaves into a ball and chop. Keeping a little back for garnish, add the coriander and basil to the salsa and stir to combine.

Roll the lemon on a chopping board to soften it and release the juices, then cut in half. Add the juice to the pan, stir and set the salsa aside to allow the flavours to infuse.

To cook the bream, heat a heavy-based frying pan over a high heat. Meanwhile, slash the skin of the fillets in 2 or 3 places. Add a dash of oil to the pan and, when really hot, add the bream fillets skin side down. Season and cook for 2–3 minutes until the fish is dark golden and the skin is crisp. (The flesh should be opaque two-thirds of the way up the fillet.)

Turn the fillets and cook on the other side for 1 minute, basting with the oil in the pan, until just cooked through.

To serve, sit the fish fillets on top of the tomato and herb salsa and sprinkle with the reserved coriander and basil.

Credit: Gordon Ramsay

POACHED LOBSTER RISOTTO
(RISOTTO AU HOMARD)
— RICK STEIN —

SERVES 4 AS A STARTER OR 2 AS A MAIN

1 cooked lobster, about 500 g
30 ml olive oil
1 shallot, finely chopped
2 cloves garlic, finely chopped
200 g carnaroli or arborio risotto rice
150 ml dry white wine
1 tbsp butter
fresh tarragon fronds, to garnish
salt and black pepper

FOR THE LOBSTER STOCK AND REDUCTION

lobster shell, chopped
1 onion, chopped
4 cloves garlic, roughly chopped, no need to peel
50 g butter
100 ml dry white wine
500 g tomatoes, roughly chopped
small handful French tarragon, roughly chopped
1.5 litres fish stock
1 tsp salt
1 tbsp Cognac
squeeze of lemon juice

Carefully remove the meat from the lobster, reserving the shell for the stock. Slice the body meat and keep the claw meat as chunky as possible.

For the stock, put the shell in a pan with the onion, garlic and 20 g of the butter. Cook for about 5 minutes over a medium heat, stirring occasionally, then add the wine, tomatoes, tarragon and stock and bring to the boil. Add the salt and leave to simmer for 40 minutes. Pass the stock through a fine sieve over another large pan and discard the solid ingredients. Keep most of the stock for the risotto, but set aside 200 ml for the reduction.

For the risotto, heat the oil in a pan, add the shallot and garlic and cook until soft. Add the rice and stir to coat it with the shallots and oil, then add the wine. Let it bubble and be absorbed by the rice, then start adding the hot stock, a ladleful at a time. Keep stirring and allow each ladleful to be absorbed before adding the next. When all the liquid has been added, taste and season as needed.

Meanwhile, finish the lobster reduction. Put the 200 ml of stock you set aside into a clean pan with the Cognac and bring to the boil. Continue to cook until it's reduced by three-quarters, then whisk in the remaining 30 g of butter to form a sauce that coats the back of a spoon. Add a squeeze of lemon juice.

Heat the tablespoon of butter in a frying pan. When it's foaming, add the lobster meat and warm it through. Serve the risotto topped with lobster meat and spoon the reduction around it. Garnish with fresh tarragon.

Credit: Maggie Beer

BEEF STROGANOFF
— MAGGIE BEER —

SERVES 4

- 80 g unsalted butter
- 20 ml extra-virgin olive oil
- 1 kg beef fillet, cut into 3 cm wide by 6.5 cm long strips
- 4 medium-sized eschalots, chopped
- 400 g mushroom, sliced
- 1 tsp grated nutmeg
- 1 cup sour cream at room temperature
- 45 ml vino cotto
- 1 tbsp lemon juice
- 2 tbsp lemon zest
- 3 tbsp fresh thyme, chopped
- freshly ground black pepper and salt flakes, to taste

Melt some of the butter in a large skillet on medium heat and add a splash of olive oil. Increase the heat to medium high, season the beef and sear the strips. Cook the beef quickly, browning on each side. You may need to work in batches. When both sides are browned, remove the beef to a bowl and set aside.

In the same pan, reduce the heat to medium, add a little more butter and the eschalots. Cook the eschalots for a minute or 2, allowing them to soak up any meat drippings. Remove the eschalots to the same bowl as the meat and set aside.

In the same pan, melt the rest of the butter with a splash of olive oil. Increase heat to medium high and add the mushrooms. Cook, stirring occasionally until the mushrooms are caramelised, but still a little firm. Grate a little nutmeg over the mushrooms, reduce the heat to low, and add the eschalots and beef back into the pan with the sour cream, stirring well to combine. Do not let it come to a simmer or the sour cream will split.

Stir in the vino cotto, add the lemon juice, lemon zest and thyme, check for seasoning and adjust if necessary.

CHICKEN COSIMA
— NIGELLA LAWSON —

SERVES 6

2½ tbsp plain flour
1 tsp ground coriander
1 tsp ground cumin
½ tsp ground turmeric
½ tsp paprika
½ tsp sea salt flakes
6 large skinless and boneless chicken thighs, cut into bite-sized chunks
15 ml cold-pressed coconut oil or regular olive oil
1 onion, peeled and chopped
500 g sweet potatoes, peeled and cut into 2–3 cm chunks
500 ml hot chicken stock
500 g cooked chickpeas (from dried) or 1 x 660 g jar chickpeas or 2 x 400 g cans chickpeas, drained
chopped fresh coriander, to serve

Preheat the oven to 200°C.

Measure the flour, spices and salt into a freezer bag and then tip in the chicken. Shake the bag around to coat the chicken with the floury spice.

Heat the oil in a wide casserole or pan (with a lid), and then fry the onion until softened but not really coloured.

Add the chicken and all the contents of the bag to the pan, and stir around for a minute or so, then add the peeled and chopped sweet potatoes and stir again.

Pour in the hot stock, then bring the pan up to the boil and tip in the drained chickpeas. Give it another good stir, then clamp on the lid and put in the oven for 25 minutes.

Check that the chicken is cooked through and the sweet potatoes are tender, then take out of the oven and leave with the lid on to stand for about 10 minutes.

Ladle into bowls, sprinkling each with chopped coriander.

Credit: Keika Oikawa

MANFREDS BEEF TARTARE
WITH MUSTARD CREAM AND WILD WATERCRESS
— CHRISTIAN PUGLISI —

SERVES 4

500 g beef inside round
fine sea salt
good olive oil
lemon juice
freshly ground black pepper

FOR THE MUSTARD CREAM

4 large eggs
80 g day-old sourdough bread (without crust)
80 ml water
90 g dijon mustard
450 ml grapeseed oil
lemon juice
fine sea salt

FOR THE CRISPY RYE BREAD

100 g rye bread
15 g clarified butter
fine sea salt

TO GARNISH

wild watercress, plucked and massaged

Prepare the Beef Tartare:
- Trim any sinew from the beef and cut it into 2x2 cm cubes.
- Season with 1.5% fine sea salt and let it rest for 1 hour.
- Place the beef in the freezer for 45 minutes until lightly frozen.
- Grind the beef using a coarse meat grinder.

Poach the eggs (for Mustard Cream):
- Use a water bath with a Roner (or sous vide) to maintain 65°C.
- Submerge eggs in their shells and poach for 35 minutes.
- Transfer immediately to cold water to cool.
- Alternatively, soft-boil the eggs for 6.5 minutes.

Make the Mustard Cream:
- Soak the sourdough bread in 80 ml water overnight.
- Blend the bread, water, poached eggs, and mustard until smooth.
- Slowly add the grapeseed oil in a thin stream while blending.
- Strain the cream and season with lemon juice and salt to taste.

Prepare the Crispy Rye Bread:
- Finely chop the rye bread.
- Toss with clarified butter and roast in the oven at 160°C for 15–20 minutes until golden and crispy.

Assemble the dish:
- Spread a generous spoonful of mustard cream onto each plate.
- Sprinkle with crispy rye bread.
- Season the tartare with olive oil, lemon juice and salt.
- Mix in plenty of wild watercress and arrange on top of the mustard cream.
- Finish with freshly ground black pepper.

RECIPES JOCK NICKED

Credit: Per-Anders Jörgensen

THAI GREEN CHICKEN CURRY
— JANE AND JIMMY BARNES —

SERVES 6

1 whole chicken

3 garlic cloves, crushed

3 coriander roots, cleaned and crushed

1 bay leaf

dash soy sauce

dash lemon juice

FOR THE CURRY

400 ml coconut milk

400 ml coconut cream

1 quantity green curry paste (see opposite)

1 tsp chicken stock powder

225 g can sliced bamboo shoots, drained

100 g pea eggplants

250 g baby eggplants, cut into quarters

1 bunch Thai basil, leaves picked

20 whole small bush chillies

10 pieces soft young coconut flesh

palm sugar, to taste

10 makrut lime leaves, very finely sliced

steamed jasmine rice, to serve

I always brine my chicken for at least 4 hours, but overnight is best. It makes the chicken plump, juicy and tasty when cooked. Anything you like the taste of can go into the brine mixture, as long as it suits the final dish. If you like a milder curry, use less curry paste. A lot of people think that nam pla (fish sauce) is used in all Thai cooking, but we use it more like salt at the table, adding it to our plates of food.

Cut the chicken into 2 legs, 2 wings and 2 thighs and cut the breasts off the carcass. Set the carcass aside for making stock (or freeze to make stock on another day).

Brine the chicken using the ingredients listed. Drain well and pat dry before using.

To make the curry, combine the coconut milk and cream in a large saucepan or wok and bring to the boil over medium heat. Add the green curry paste and chicken stock powder. Reduce the heat to medium–low and simmer for 15 minutes, stirring now and again, until reduced slightly.

Add all the chicken pieces except for the breast. Cook for 20 minutes. Slice the breast meat, add to the pan and cook for a further 10 minutes.

Stir in the bamboo shoots and leave bubbling away for 10 minutes. Add the eggplants and half the basil leaves. Cook for a further 10 minutes then turn off the heat. You can add the chillies and coconut flesh now.

Make sure you taste the sauce as you go along; if it's too hot just add a little palm sugar to balance it out, or if it needs to be saltier just add salt.

Stir in the lime leaves. Transfer to a serving bowl and scatter with the remaining basil leaves. Serve with rice.

NOTE: Look for young coconut flesh and bush chillies at Asian grocery stores. You may find fresh bamboo shoots too. Makrut lime leaves are often known as kaffir lime leaves.

GREEN CURRY PASTE

- 4 cm knob young ginger
- 4 cm knob galangal
- 2 cm knob turmeric
- 2 lemongrass stalks
- peel of 1 makrut lime
- 4 makrut lime leaves, chopped
- 2 garlic cloves
- 4 coriander roots, cleaned
- string of fresh green peppercorns (see note)
- 2 small red eschalots
- 6 long green chillies
- sea salt
- 1 tsp shrimp paste

You will need a mortar and pestle for this – you can get them from most Asian grocery stores. I have a large, heavy, stone one.

Chop the ginger, galangal, turmeric and lemongrass into small chunks and start pounding in the mortar and pestle with the makrut peel and leaves. I begin with the tougher, stringier ingredients, as they take a bit more pounding than the softer ones.

Once the mixture starts becoming paste-like, chop the other ingredients, add and pound in. Salt generously – the crystals will help cut through the fibres and pulp. Add shrimp paste at the end and mix in well. I find my paste is never as smooth as bought paste, but I'm really happy with that.

NOTE: *Fresh green peppercorns are available from Asian grocers and some large greengrocers. Alternatively use 1 tablespoon canned green peppercorns.*

Credit: Alan Benson Photography

DAMPER AND LAMB BUTTER
— RESTAURANT ORANA —

MAKES 10 PORTIONS

FOR THE LAMB BUTTER

250 g diced lamb fat from the butcher	
100 ml water	
3 large sprigs rosemary	
half bunch thyme	
½ head garlic	
2 tsp salt	
1 tsp white pepper, freshly ground	
4 egg yolks	
2 tsp apple cider vinegar	
1 tbsp white soy sauce	
½ tsp salt	
0.5 g xanthan gum (you can buy this in the supermarket)	

FOR THE DAMPER

- 200 g bread flour
- 50 g wholewheat flour
- 140 ml water
- 20 g sourdough mother
- 3.4 g compressed yeast
- 40 g potato mash
- 1½ tsp salt

Start by making the lamb butter. Get your pan to a medium–high heat, add in your diced lamb, and stir it constantly. You want to begin to caramelise it, and lots of the fat will start being released. This will take about 2 minutes. Then add in the water, herbs, garlic, 2 tsp salt and pepper, turn the heat to low and the fat will slowly start to render. Leave it on this low heat for about 20 minutes to fully render. You'll know it's ready when you can't see any chunks of lamb and all the water has evaporated. At this stage, pass it through a fine strainer or coffee filter to remove the solids.

Now add the egg yolks, apple cider vinegar, white soy and ½ tsp salt into a metal bowl and place it over a pot of simmering water. Whisk until it's doubled in size and is light and airy (about 4 minutes). Then slowly add in the lamb fat mixture while you're whisking (the lamb fat should be at 60°C). As it starts to thicken, add in 5–10 ml of warm water, then continue adding the lamb fat mixture until it's all incorporated into the egg yolk mix. Add the xanthan gum and mix through (this step is useful if you are putting it into a cream charger, otherwise it's not essential).

You then have two options: put it into a dip or side bowl (it will be more like the consistency of a hollandaise sauce) or a cream gun with two cream chargers, shaking vigorously after each one. Then keep in a warm place as close to 50°C as you can.

To make the damper, fix a bread dough hook into your mixer. Add the flours, water, mother and yeast and mix until combined. Add the potato and mix until fully combined, then continue to mix for another 10 minutes. Add the salt and mix for 10 more minutes. Scoop the dough out of the bowl and place on an oiled tray to let it rise. Once it has risen about 30–40% divide the dough into 10 even pieces and rest for 20 minutes. At this point, roll each piece into a ball and let it prove in a warm spot for 2 hours.

Once proved, stretch the dough out slightly so you can wrap it around a stick. At Restaurant Orana we used a eucalyptus branch, but you could use a wooden skewer. Cover with a tea towel and let rest for 2 hours. Then you're ready to cook them – place them over the coals of a hibachi or in your pizza oven. If you can't do either of those, you could pan-fry them in a small amount of oil. You'll know they're ready when they look golden and crisp. Serve with the lamb butter.

RECIPES JOCK NICKED

Credit: Matt Turner

Credit: Lauren Zonfrillo

INDEX

Allen, Andy 248
almonds
   almond cantucci 235
   broccoli, jalapeño and smoked almond salad 179
   torta Caprese 219
anchovies
   anchovy and guancile toast 213
   bagna cauda with crudités and crunchy bread 121
   Caesar salad with leftover roast chicken 166
Aperol sour 106
apple
   Jock's apple tarte tatin 220
apricot
   grilled stone fruit with waffles and salted butterscotch sauce 61
arancini, tomato with basil and mortadella 132
Ava's vegan burger 72
avocado
   avocado salsa 51
   spicy guacamole 159

baby gem with spicy guacamole 159
bagna cauda with crudités and crunchy bread 121
baked Italian eggs 40
banana bread with Alfie 223
barbecue lamb and beetroot salad 187
barbecued eggplant with quinoa and basil salad 192
Barnes, Jimmy and Jane 260

basil
   barbecued eggplant with quinoa and basil salad 192
   basil oil 176
   pesto 34
   tomato arancini with basil and mortadella 126
beans, green
   Niçoise salad 184
beans, white
   Italian cannellini bean salad with poached chicken 155
   pasta e fagioli con cavolo nero 79
beef
   beef stroganoff 255
   cottage pie 86
   crispy shredded beef 139
   Manfreds beef tartare 258
   square sausage 47
   steak sandwich with smoky pepper glaze 156
   the perfect steak 89
Beer, Maggie 255
beetroot
   Ava's vegan burger 72
   barbecue lamb and beetroot salad 187
   marinated beetroot 187
berries
   summer berries with Greek yoghurt and pistachio praline 240
   summer fruit crumble with coconut ice cream 216
bircher porridge 38

biscuits
   almond cantucci 235
   traditional Scottish shortbread 230
black pepper mud crab 98
branston pickle 16
bread
   anchovy and guancile toast 213
   banana bread with Alfie 223
   cottage cheese and spinach pockets with spiced honey 136
   damper and lamb butter 262
   focaccia with semi-dried tomatoes, olives and rosemary 116
   Glasgow rolls 46
   naan 95
   tortillas 43
bread and butter pickles 15
breakfast
   baked Italian eggs 40
   bircher porridge 38
   breakfast tortillas 43
   Campari-cured gravlax with lemon cottage cheese sauce 52
   chilli coffee eggs 58
   corn fritters with egg and avocado salsa 51
   crepes with salted butterscotch sauce 67
   fluffy coconut pancakes with mango salsa 62
   Glasgow rolls 46
   green breakfast salad with farro and tahini verde 57

grilled stone fruit with waffles and salted butterscotch sauce 61
scrambled eggs with 'nduja and leftover pizza dough 49
square sausage 47
tattie scones 48
breakfast tortillas 43
broccoli, jalapeño and smoked almond salad 179
bugs
    salt and pepper bugs 130
bumble bees 238
burger
    Ava's vegan burger 72
butter
    Cafe de Paris butter 23
    damper and lamb butter 262
    homemade butter 31
butterscotch sauce, salted 61, 67

Caesar salad with leftover roast chicken 166
Cafe de Paris butter 23
cake
    blood orange and negroni cake 224
    carrot cake 226
    lemon drizzle cake 232
    torta Caprese 219
Campari
    Campari cassatelle 236
    Campari-cured gravlax with lemon cottage cheese sauce 52
capsicum
    piperade 145
carrot
    candied carrot 226
    carrot cake 226
cavolo nero
    pasta e fagioli con cavolo nero 79
celery
    pea, cucumber and celery salad 158
cheese
    cottage cheese and spinach pockets with spiced honey 136
    cream cheese icing 226
    lemon cottage cheese sauce 52
    mac 'n cottage cheese 84
    spaghetti carbonara 80
    super-simple homemade ricotta 20

tomato arancini with basil and mortadella 126
tomato salad with grilled peach, fresh ricotta and lemon granita 176
zingy zucchini and parmesan salad 188
chicken
    butter chicken 94
    Caesar salad with leftover roast chicken 166
    chicken cosima 256
    chicken liver parfait 247
    chicken tikka 94
    fermented chilli glazed chicken 248
    Italian cannellini bean salad with poached chicken 155
    limoncello chicken traybake 101
    southern fried chicken 90
    Thai green chicken curry 260
    ultimate roast chicken 105
chickpeas
    vegan chickpea gnocchi sardi 150
chilli
    broccoli, jalapeño and smoked almond salad 179
    chilli coffee eggs 58
    chilli oil crab noodles 142
    fermented chilli glazed chicken 248
    5-minute crispy chilli oil 12
    wood-fired scallops with jalapeño and lime 206
chips, triple-cooked 125
chocolate
    bumble bees 238
    torta Caprese 219
classic sausage rolls 148
cocktail garnishes 105
cocktails
    Aperol sour 106
    negroni 107
    vesper martini 106
coconut
    bumble bees 238
    coconut ice cream 216
    fluffy coconut pancakes with mango salsa 62
    summer fruit crumble with coconut ice cream 216
coffee
    chilli coffee eggs 58s

corn fritters with egg and avocado salsa 51
cottage cheese
    Campari-cured gravlax with lemon cottage cheese sauce 52
    cottage cheese and spinach pockets with spiced honey 136
    lemon cottage cheese sauce 52
    mac 'n cottage cheese 84
crab
    black pepper mud crab 98
    chilli oil crab noodles 142
cream cheese icing 226
crepes with salted butterscotch sauce 67
crispy shredded beef 139
croutons 172
    panzanella salad with the ultimate croutons 182
cucumber
    bread and butter pickles 15
    panzanella salad with the ultimate croutons 182
    pea, cucumber and celery salad 158
curry
    butter chicken 94
    green curry paste 261
    Thai green chicken curry 260

damper and lamb butter 262
desserts
    almond cantucci 235
    banana bread with Alfie 223
    blood orange and negroni cake 224
    bumble bees 238
    Campari cassatelle 236
    carrot cake 226
    Jock's apple tarte tatin 220
    lemon drizzle cake 232
    summer berries with Greek yoghurt and pistachio praline 240
    summer fruit crumble with coconut ice cream 216
    torta Caprese 219
    traditional Scottish shortbread 230
dressing
    broccoli, jalapeño and smoked almond salad, for 179

INDEX

Caesar salad, for 166
Niçoise salad, for 184
tahini verde dressing 55
vinaigrette 159
zingy zucchini and parmesan salad, for 188

easy Niçoise salad 184
eggplant
   barbecued eggplant with quinoa and basil salad 192
eggs
   baked Italian eggs 40
   breakfast tortillas 43
   Caesar salad with leftover roast chicken 166
   chilli coffee eggs 58
   corn fritters with egg and avocado salsa 51
   green breakfast salad with farro and tahini verde 57
   piperade 145
   scrambled eggs with 'nduja and leftover pizza dough 49
   spaghetti carbonara 80

farro
   green breakfast salad with farro and tahini verde 57
fish
   Campari-cured gravlax with lemon cottage cheese sauce 52
   harissa tuna with roasted vegetable salad 170
   Niçoise salad 184
   spaghetti with swordfish polpette 76
   whole roasted king dory 201
'fish' sauce, vegan 25
focaccia
   incredibly easy with semi-dried tomatoes, olives and rosemary 116
   pizzetta 202
fritters
   corn fritters with egg and avocado salsa 51
fruit
   summer fruit crumble with coconut ice cream 216
   ultimate roast chicken 105

Glasgow rolls 46
gnoccho fritto with shaved mortadella 129
gravlax
   Campari-cured gravlax with lemon cottage cheese sauce 52
green breakfast salad with farro and tahini verde 57
green curry paste 261
gremolata 122
grilled stone fruit with waffles and salted butterscotch sauce 61
guacamole, spicy 159
guanciale
   piperade 145
   spaghetti carbonara 80

herbs
   basil oil 176
   focaccia with semi-dried tomatoes, olives and rosemary 116
   gremolata 122
   pesto 34
   salsa verde 20
   tahini verde dressing 57
   tomato and herb salsa 250
   tomato arancini with basil and mortadella 126
homemade butter 31
honey
   cottage cheese and spinach pockets with spiced honey 136

ice cream
   coconut ice cream 216
icing
   cream cheese icing 226
Italian cannellini bean salad with poached chicken 155

jalapeño
   broccoli, jalapeño and smoked almond salad 179
   wood-fired scallops with jalapeño and lime 206
Jock's apple tarte tatin 220

kimchi
   speck and prawn kimchi fried rice 134
king dory, whole roasted 201
King's cut whisky 107

lamb
   barbecue lamb and beetroot salad 187
   damper and lamb butter 262
Lawson, Nigella 256
lemon
   lemon cottage cheese sauce 52
   lemon drizzle cake 232
   lemon granita 176
lettuce
   baby gem with spicy guacamole 159
   bistro salad with Jock's French dressing 165
   Caesar salad with leftover roast chicken 166
   classic vinaigrette salad 159
lime
   wood-fired scallops with jalapeño and lime 206
limoncello chicken traybake 101
lobster risotto, poached 253

mac 'n cottage cheese 84
Manfreds beef tartare 258
mango salsa 62
meatballs
   mondeghili meatballs with gremolata 122
mondeghili meatballs with gremolata 122
mortadella
   gnoccho fritto with shaved mortadella 129
   tomato arancini with basil and mortadella 126
mozzarella
   tomato arancini with basil and mortadella 126
mustard cream 258

naan 95
negroni 107
   blood orange and negroni cake 224
   negroni sticky pork ribs 198
Niçoise salad 184
noodles
   chilli oil crab noodles 142

oats
   bircher porridge 38

oil
   basil oil 176
   5-minute crispy chilli oil 12
   preserving oil (semi-dried tomatoes) 18
Oliver, Jamie 244
olives
   focaccia with semi-dried tomatoes, olives and rosemary 116
   Pacific oysters with Sicilian olive mignonette 110
   panzanella salad with the ultimate croutons 182
   stuffed fried Sicilian olives 113
orange
   blood orange and negroni cake 224
oysters
   Pacific oysters with Sicilian olive mignonette 110

Pacific oysters with Sicilian olive mignonette 110
pancakes
   crepes with salted butterscotch sauce 67
   fluffy coconut pancakes with mango salsa 62
panzanella salad with the ultimate croutons 182
parmesan
   zingy zucchini and parmesan salad 188
parsley
   gremolata 122
pasta
   mac 'n cottage cheese 84
   pasta e fagioli con cavolo nero 79
   spaghetti carbonara 80
   spaghetti with swordfish polpette 76
   vegan chickpea gnocchi sardi 150
pastries
   Campari cassatelle 236
pea, cucumber and celery salad 158
peaches
   grilled stone fruit with waffles and salted butterscotch sauce 61
   tomato salad with grilled peach, fresh ricotta and lemon granita 176

pesto 34
   wild garlic 244
pickles
   branston pickle 16
   bread and butter pickles 15
pie
   cottage pie 86
piperade 145
pistachio
   pistachio praline 240
   summer berries with Greek yoghurt and pistachio praline 240
pizzetta 202
poached lobster risotto 253
porchetta 205
pork
   classic sausage rolls 148
   mondeghili meatballs with gremolata 122
   negroni sticky pork ribs 198
   porchetta 205
   spicy pork skewers with summer chopped salad 210
   square sausage 47
porridge, bircher 38
potatoes
   cottage pie 86
   tattie scones 48
   triple-cooked chips 125
prawn
   speck and prawn kimchi fried rice 134
   Thai barbecue prawns 194
Puglisi, Christian 258

quinoa
   barbecued eggplant with quinoa and basil salad 192

Ramsay, Gordon 250
Restaurant Orana 262
ribs
   negroni sticky pork ribs 198
rice
   risotto verde with agrodolce 146
   speck and prawn kimchi fried rice 134
ricotta
   super-simple homemade ricotta 20
   tomato salad with grilled peach, fresh ricotta and lemon granita 176

risotto
   poached lobster risotto 253
   risotto verde with agrodolce 146
rolls
   Glasgow rolls 46
rosemary
   focaccia with semi-dried tomatoes, olives and rosemary 116

salad
   baby gem with spicy guacamole 159
   barbecue lamb and beetroot salad 187
   barbecued eggplant with quinoa and basil salad 192
   bistro salad with Jock's French dressing 165
   broccoli, jalapeño and smoked almond salad 179
   Caesar salad with leftover roast chicken 166
   classic vinaigrette salad 159
   green breakfast salad with farro and tahini verde 57
   harissa tuna with roasted vegetable salad 170
   Italian cannellini bean salad with poached chicken 155
   Niçoise salad 184
   panzanella salad with the ultimate croutons 182
   pea, cucumber and celery salad 158
   squid salad with cassava crackers 174
   summer chopped salad 210
   tomato salad with grilled peach, fresh ricotta and lemon granita 176
   zingy zucchini and parmesan salad 188
salmon
   Campari-cured gravlax with lemon cottage cheese sauce 52
   stuffed roasted salmon 244
salsa
   avocado salsa 41
   breakfast tortillas, for 43
   mango salsa 62
   tomato and herb 250

salsa verde 20
   risotto verde with agrodolce 146
salt and pepper bugs 130
salted butterscotch sauce 61, 67
sandwich
   steak sandwich with smoky pepper glaze 156
sauces and condiments
   bagna cauda with crudités and crunchy bread 121
   branston pickle 16
   bread and butter pickles 15
   butter chicken sauce, for 94
   fermented chilli sauce 248
   5-minute crispy chilli oil 12
   gremolata 122
   lemon cottage cheese sauce 52
   pesto 34
   salsa verde 20
   smoky pepper beer glaze 156
   sugo al pomodoro 28
   vegan 'fish' sauce 25
sausage, square 47
sausage rolls, classic 148
scallops
   wood-fired scallops with jalapeño and lime 206
Scottish shortbread, traditional 230
Scottish pie 86
sea bream with tomato and herb salsa 250
seafood
   black pepper mud crab 98
   Campari-cured gravlax with lemon cottage cheese sauce 52
   chilli oil crab noodles 142
   harissa tuna with roasted vegetable salad 170
   Niçoise salad 184
   Pacific oysters with Sicilian olive mignonette 110
   poached lobster risotto 259
   salt and pepper bugs 130
   sea bream with tomato and herb salsa 250
   spaghetti with swordfish polpette 76
   speck and prawn kimchi fried rice 134
   squid salad with cassava crackers 174
   stuffed roasted salmon 244

Thai barbecue prawns 194
whole roasted king dory 201
wood-fired scallops with jalapeño and lime 206
semi-dried tomatoes 26
shortbread, traditional Scottish 230
skewers
   spicy pork skewers with summer chopped salad 210
smoky pepper beer glaze 156
soup
   pasta e fagioli con cavolo nero 79
southern fried chicken 90
spaghetti carbonara 80
spaghetti with swordfish polpette 76
speck and prawn kimchi fried rice 134
spinach
   cottage cheese and spinach pockets with spiced honey 136
   sautéed spinach with Dijon 158
square sausage 47
squid salad with cassava crackers 174
steak
   steak sandwich with smoky pepper glaze 156
   the perfect steak 89
Stein, Rick 253
stroganoff, beef 255
stuffed fried Sicilian olives 113
stuffed roasted salmon 244
sugo al pomodoro 28
summer berries with Greek yoghurt and pistachio praline 240
summer chopped salad 210
summer fruit crumble with coconut ice cream 216
super-simple homemade ricotta 20
sweet potato
   Ava's vegan burger 72
swordfish
   spaghetti with swordfish polpette 76

tahini verde dressing 57
tarte tatin
   Jock's apple tarte tatin 220
tattie scones 48
Thai barbecue prawns 194
Thai green chicken curry 260

the perfect steak 89
toast
   anchovy and guancile toast 213
tomatoes
   baked Italian eggs 40
   focaccia with semi-dried tomatoes, olives and rosemary 116
   panzanella salad with the ultimate croutons 182
   semi-dried tomatoes 26
   sugo al pomodoro 28
   tomato and herb salsa 260
   tomato salad with grilled peach, fresh ricotta and lemon granita 176
torta Caprese 219
tortillas, breakfast 43
traditional Scottish shortbread 230
triple-cooked chips 125
tuna
   harissa tuna with roasted vegetable salad 170
   Niçoise salad 184

vegan
   Ava's vegan burger 72
   vegan chickpea gnocchi sardi 150
   vegan 'fish' sauce 25
vegetables
   bagna cauda with crudités and crunchy bread 121
   harissa tuna with roasted vegetable salad 170
vesper martini 106
vinaigrette 159

waffles
   grilled stone fruit with waffles and salted butterscotch sauce 61
whisky 107
White, Marco Pierre 247
wood-fired scallops with jalapeño and lime 206

zingy zucchini and parmesan salad 188
zucchini
   zingy zucchini and parmesan salad 188

RECIPES TO REMEMBER
First published in Australia in 2025 by
Simon & Schuster (Australia) Pty Limited
Level 4, 32 York St, Sydney NSW 2000

10 9 8 7 6 5 4 3 2 1

New York Amsterdam/Antwerp London Toronto Sydney New Delhi
Visit our website at www.simonandschuster.com.au

© Jock Zonfrillo 2025

All rights reserved. No part of this publication may be reproduced, stored in a retrieval system, or transmitted in any form or by any means, electronic, mechanical, photocopying, recording or otherwise, without prior permission of the publisher.

 A catalogue record for this book is available from the National Library of Australia

ISBN: 9781761631917

Cover and internal design: Daniel New
Cover and internal food photography: Rob Palmer
Back cover image: Tina Smigielski
Extra food photography: Jock Zonfrillo
All additional photography: Lauren and Jock Zonfrillo
Food Styling: Vanessa Austin
Cooking: Dixie Elliott and Tina McLeish
Printed and bound in China by Asia Pacific Offset Limited

Every effort has been made to contact all copyright owners to ensure that their contribution is properly acknowledged. Where we have been unable, despite our best endeavours, to make contact we would welcome hearing from anyone concerned, so that we may include an appropriate acknowledgement in any reprints.

NOTE TO READER: This publication includes historical photographs of Indigenous individuals. We recognise the importance of cultural sensitivity and invite feedback from the community.